FROM GARLIC GULCH

A TRUE AMERICAN STORY

David E. Svendsen

2008

Photographs from the personal collection of the author.

ISBN: 978-1-934733-22-6

Revised October 2008

SPECIAL THANKS

TO DANA ELKUN, POET, SCHOLAR, EDITOR
AND NEW FRIEND

THIS BOOK IS DEDICATED TO MY FRIEND AND MENTOR VINE DELORIA JR.

Most of all, in his memory.

There have been many very important people in my life, but none more important than Vine Deloria Jr. My life changed when I walked into his classroom and over the years of our friendship. I came to understand how important the truth is to a people's survival and how devastating and destructive lies, treachery, and deceit are to that same survival. With Vine's help I came to see the world through a different pair of eyes, eyes that helped me understand how we human beings should be treating each other as opposed to how we have been treating each other for centuries.

I learned from my friend: "We can be intelligent without being wise, but we can't be wise without being intelligent." And: "We can be brave without being courageous, but we can't be courageous without being brave." Without this understanding of life and the strength it has given me, I could have never taken a job as Civil Rights Investigator; I wouldn't have understood the importance of correcting past transgressions and making people's lives better. These lessons are something too many people in leadership today still don't understand.

When I last saw my friend, we discussed this book and he gave me the wisdom to see its value to my family and friends as well as the courage to write it.

TABLE OF CONTENTS

INTRODUCTION

I was born on Thursday, February 2, 1939 (Groundhog Day) at 11:10am at Seattle General Hospital in Seattle, Washington. Our family lived at 5232 Orchard Terrace, which was in an area called Garlic Gulch because of the Italian influence. That address was my home for the next 19 years. I haven't the slightest clue as to why I was born. Oh, I know the biological why. I just don't know the spiritual why. I know where my fingers and toes came from, the color of my eyes and the reason I am going bald why. I just don't know where my soul came from or where it's going. I guess that's what this is all about. I've been very lucky in many, many ways and not so lucky in others. There are some great and not so great people in my family. I've had some of the best friends anyone could possibly wish for. This book is for my yesterday family, my now family and my family yet to come, as well as for all my friends past, present, and future.

I am in my late sixties now, and I have some things to say to my family and friends. Things I have experienced and how they have affected me. I have two goals with this writing. First, I want them to know just how important they have all been to me, and this seems the best way to do it. I have always had a great interest in history. I wish someone in my family, on either my mother's or father's side, had written down what their lives were like. Big things, little things, how they felt about the world they lived in. What was daily life like? How did they feel about their family and friends? As far as I am aware, no one ever did. So, my second goal is to do just that: to leave a written record for my grandchildren and their children, their children's children, etc. My fondest wish is that they will enjoy reading about life in the middle and end of the twentieth century. At least how life was for me, in the world I grew up in.

I am the last of six children of Sigurd Dagmar Swensen and Bertha Longden Swensen. I have three sisters and two brothers. One brother and two sisters are now deceased. My dad was forty-seven and my mother forty-five when I was born. Katherine Dale is my oldest sister. Then there is Shirley "Toodie" and Martha Jane, Harry Longden and Forrest Grant, and I am the last. Harry died a few years ago, Jane in 2004. I've been married twice, first to Autumn and then to Carol. I have four children: three girls,

Candie Lynn, Kristin Heidi, Cary Lee, and a boy, David Jr. I have four grandchildren, two girls, Rachel and Gracie, and two boys, Mitchell and Jesse. More about them as we go. I also have some world-class friends. There's Richard, Robert, Ricardo, George, Billy and Marge, two Frank's, Rhonda, Fred, Jack and Gail, Barbara, David, Jill, Vine and Barbara, Lew and Suzy, Jerry and many others who have come and gone in my life but still remain my friends and always will. The difference between one's love for family and one's love for friends is that your family will always be your family. Nothing can change that, good or bad. Friends, on the other hand, are all volunteers and they can quit being your friend anytime you or they choose to. I've done some stupid things in my life and lost some friends that I shouldn't have lost and now miss. I can think of two Andy's, Paul, Mary, Rhoda, Myrna, Bettye and others I will mention later. Maybe we all need to screw up once in a while so we can grasp the meaning of regret and try not to make the same mistakes over again. At least that's the way it's been in my life. I'm just grateful for the friends I do have and hope to pay tribute to them in this writing.

Then of course there are the family members we can do without and those who have crossed our paths and left turbulence in their wake. We need them in our lives too. There's my sister Dale and my brother Harry. People with whom I've worked with or done business, like Virginia, Douglas, Lennox, Jerry, Yvonne, John, Phil and others, also to be mentioned later. They all help us realize just what a gift we have in our loved ones, family and friends.

Then there are the heroes and villains, people whom we don't know personally but who affect our everyday lives. When I first meet someone, sooner or later I get around to asking who his or her heroes are. You can learn a great deal about someone by knowing whom he or she admires. Most of the time I can tell if I want to continue the relationship or not from that one question. Not always though. For example, I have chosen to pursue friendships even after someone told me they admired Jesus the most. I certainly do not think of Jesus as a villain. However, I know for sure that some who claim to love Jesus are in fact villains themselves, clear to the bone. I even have a few friends who think Ronald Reagan was a great President.

CHAPTER ONE: 1939 to 1952

Like I said, I was born in 1939. I don't remember a thing until I was about five or six, around 1944. World War II was in full rage, and the Greatest Generation was changing the world we were going to live in forever. By the time I could remember anything, it was just my brother Forrest and I left at home. My father was working at Todd Shipyards and my mother was a neighborhood air raid warden. We lived at 5232 Orchard Terrace, and all of our neighbors had dark curtains on their windows. Every time the air raid siren would go off, I would run and hide under my parents' bed. My mother would pull all the curtains closed, put on her air raid warden helmet and go up the court to make sure no light was leaking out from our neighbors' windows. If there was any light, she would have to go to the door and make sure it was put out. I didn't come out from under the bed until the "all clear" was sounded and my mother re-opened the curtains.

My first friend was Richard Fenkner who lived across the alley in back of our house. His father also worked for Todd Shipyards. We played cars and war with our other friends in the neighborhood: Loran, Punky and Bobby. When we played war, we would march around singing, "Praise the Lord and Pass the Ammunition." Then we would "kill" hundreds of "dirty Japs" or "stinking Krauts." When we played cowboys and Indians, we "killed" as many "dirty Indians" as we could in the time allotted or before our mothers called us home for dinner. It was always "dirty Jap and dirty Indian" and a whole lot worse. That's what we heard at the dinner table and around the neighborhood. When V-E Day came, the whole neighborhood erupted. People came out of their houses banging pots and pans, firing guns and setting off firecrackers. It was the same for V-J Day. I remember the newspaper headlines, in big bold letters, "WAR ENDS IN EUROPE" and "JAPS SURRENDER." At the time I didn't know anything about the atomic bomb, nor did I care. All I knew was I didn't have to run and hide under the bed anymore. I didn't have to be afraid of the Japs and the Krauts. The Indians I wasn't sure about.

My kids don't believe me, and sometimes it is hard for me to imagine, but I remember a life before computers, cell phones, pagers and televisions, before supermarkets, malls, mega drugs, Cineplex's, even freeways.

We did our grocery shopping at the Red and White grocery store and Reid's Meat Market on the corner of Othello and Rainier Avenue. Across the street was Mankee's Drug Store and Soda Fountain. There was also Mondo's Meats on the corner of Genesee and Rainier. My mother would buy meat there on her way home from her job at the Bon Marche.

Even after the war had ended, there were a lot of residual factors in our lives. My mother had gotten a job in the shipping department at the Bon Marche in downtown Seattle because all the men were off fighting in Europe and the Pacific. When the men came home, most of the women workers were fired and sent back to the kitchen without so much as a "thank you." Somehow my mother was able to keep her position; she continued to work at the Bon well into her seventies and even part-time into her eighties. During the war, everything had been rationed, well, nearly everything: meat, gas, tires, sugar, things like that. Some things were exempt from rationing, like calf brains, tongue, pig knuckles, liver. My mother was a great cook, so even after the war we kept on eating the same things. Jean Beal, who lived behind us, had a "victory garden," which nearly everyone did during the war, except my mother. She hated getting her hands dirty. So she and Mrs. Beal made a deal: Jean would raise fruits and vegetables and my mother would can them. Things like beans, corn, squash, cucumbers for pickles. She would also can peaches, pears, berries for jam and make apple sauce. There were no supermarkets then, so you couldn't just run to the store and get anything out of season. No cargo planes flew from Peru with fresh fruit and vegetables in December or January. You either canned them yourself for use over the winter or sometimes you could find canned items in the local grocery store. But they weren't very good. I think we ate healthier then and maybe it's not a bad idea to go back to. Especially if you think about the processed junk they are feeding us now. Everything contains pesticides, antibiotics, steroids, trans fats or other such unhealthy chemicals. Who knows what it is doing to us? I sure don't.

Our main entertainment was the radio, Sunday's newspaper and the two small theaters, one in Hillman City and one in Columbia City. Kids in the neighborhood could go to a movie theater for a Saturday afternoon double feature for 25 cents. So on Saturdays my mother would give me a quarter for the movie and a nickel or dime for some popcorn or candy. On the radio we would listen to "Lux Radio Theater," "Burns and Allen," "The

Lone Ranger," "The Shadow," "Jack Benny," "The Cisco Kid," "The Green Hornet" and many, many other great radio shows. At my age then, I didn't pay much attention to the news. But my father listened to Walter Winchell every night. And we all looked forward to the Sunday newspaper. My brother and I would fight over the comics while my mother and father divided up the rest of the paper.

When I was about eight, my mother signed me up for Cub Scouts at our local Presbyterian Church. I hated it. All we did was listen to bible stories being read to us or paint plaster-of-paris faces of Jesus. My friend Richard, who attended St. Edwards Catholic Church, saved me when I became old enough to join the Boy Scouts. His school had a troop, so I joined Troop 222. There was one problem. Everyone in our neighborhood who was not Catholic believed the church basement was full of guns to take over the United States whenever the Pope told them to do so. My first meeting at St. Edwards was in the basement of the church and try as I may, I couldn't find any guns. Kids in the neighborhood said they were there, they were just well hidden. I met some great friends there: Jerry Banchero, whose father owned the meat market that my mother sent me to, and Dale Bond, who gave me a ride to school most every day. Our troop leader was a man named Harvey.

One weekend we went on a camping and fishing trip out to the Green River. On Sunday morning everyone went to church. Since I was the only non-Catholic in the troop, they left me behind to watch the camp. We were allowed three fish each per day, and there were six of us. While they were at church, I caught 18 trout. I was really pleased with myself, until they got back. They were ready to kill me, but Harvey stepped in and suggested we eat the evidence and bury the bones. Then everyone but me could get back to fishing. We did that and everyone else fished the whole rest of the day. No one caught a single fish. I was lucky to escape with my life. I still hear about it to this very day. All during my years in this troop no one ever suggested that I should become Catholic or that I had to believe in God. I was just accepted as is.

In 1950 I was eleven and along came the worst winter in Seattle history. We had three feet of snow in our front yard and it lasted for several weeks. We had lots of hills in our neighborhood and everyone's parents went out and bought them sleds. I asked my dad to get me a sled, so he went out to the garage, found some old runners and an ironing board. He made me a sled with an imprint of an iron right in the middle of the board. There was no time to get it painted. When I showed up, I was the laughing stock of the neighborhood. That is, until we started to sled down the best hill around. The hill was on a piece of property owned by a doctor. It was at least a football field long and ended right at the lake. My sled was so fast, everyone wanted a turn on it. When you reached the end of the run, you had to roll off the sled to keep from going into the lake. We all told Punky that and were yelling at him to roll off the sled when he got to the bottom. He didn't and sailed a good three feet off the bank and into the lake. Shortly after that I got pneumonia and had to stay inside until the snow was gone. I never saw my sled again.

Before the war my father sold Nash cars for Lamping Motor on Capitol Hill. Since there were no cars to sell after the war, my father went into business for himself selling printing machinery under the name Swensen-Case Company. Bob Case was married to my oldest sister Dale. I have no idea how his name came to be on my father's letterhead because as far as I know he never had anything to do with the business. Bob used to take my brother and I fishing and I worshiped him. I thought he was the neatest guy. It was only after many years that I learned about the real Bob and how I had misplaced my trust in him.

I entered the first grade at Brighton Grade School in 1945. There were no school buses then, so I walked to school with a bunch of other grade schoolers, kids from first through eighth grades. Every day I carried a lunch in a brown paper bag, which my mother prepared. It was always the same: a peanut butter and jelly sandwich on white bread and an apple, orange or banana. I also carried a nickel for milk. I often skipped the milk and got a candy bar at a little store on the way home. Since my friend Richard went to St. Edwards Catholic School, I didn't see him until after school and during the summer breaks when we would pal around with Loran, Bobby and Punky. Bobby was a little older and also went to St. Edwards. As I recall, one summer we had a World Championship Spitting Contest, and Punky won hands down. I think the record was twelve feet, six and a half inches. That was with the wind at his back. Richard's father was a heavy smoker. Richard would come up with some cigarettes now and then, and we would sneak into an apple orchard and smoke up. His father died of a heart attack when Richard and I were about eight. I felt really bad for Richard, his brothers and sister. However, we just kept on sneaking into the apple orchard and smoking whenever we could. It seemed like cigarettes were easier to get than candy.

When they were getting ready to build the nation's first mall out at Northgate in 1946, my father bought a five-room tract house where the mall was going to go. He and some of my brother Harry's friends gutted the house and moved it into our backyard. They were all recently out of the service and needed the work. Of course, my brother Harry was nowhere around when there was work to be done. My father turned that house into a garage and workshop; it is still there to this day. My father built the garage door out of aluminum and magnesium. When he finished and had the door hung, he started swearing up a storm. Now, when my father swore he used words like "judice priest," "by golly" and "gee wiz." He was mad because when he measured the door, he was off by one sixty-fourth of an inch on the corners of the door. When you looked at the door you couldn't help but notice there was no door handle anywhere. To open the door you simply walked up to it and used one finger in the middle and about three-quarters the way up and pushed. The door swung open. It was so finely balanced that it took very little pressure to open it. To lock it there was a nail on the inside that you put into a hole to block the door from opening, and a side door with a key lock. Like our house it was never locked.

Ours was an interesting neighborhood. There were two blocks between Seward Park Avenue and Lake Washington, divided by 55th Avenue. We lived on the west side of 55th Avenue, and all of the homes on the east side of 55th were waterfront. Those homes were huge estates with long driveways, acres of lawn and gardens, large docks with expensive boats. In 1949 a doctor and his family moved into one of these large estates. They had three boys. One was a few years older than us, one our age and one younger. It didn't take the rest of us long to make friends with the one our age, Paul, or Chippo as he was called. We soon had an invitation to go swimming with Chippo everyday at 4:00 p.m., provided that one of our mothers agreed to watch us if Chippo's mother couldn't. Also, it was part of the deal that we would help Chippo with chores like mowing the lawn. We all thought that was great. Their yard was so big it had two tennis courts and an area large enough for us to play baseball between the house and the lake. Unlike today, we didn't have fathers trying to make professional athletes out of us. We just made up our own rules as we played. Mowing and raking their lawn was an all-day job. By 4:00 p.m. we were ready for a swim.

There was one particularly hot summer day when we got finished with the lawn mowing and then went home to get our swimsuits. When we got back, Chippo's mother came out and said we couldn't go swimming because she had some kind of appointment and none of the other mothers were available to watch us. We were all disappointed and ended up in Bobby's garage. Every now and then, ten-year-olds do stupid things. This was one of those thens. Bobby's dad owned the Virginia V, the last of the old passenger steam ships that used to take people around Puget Sound before roads were built. Passenger boats were required by Coast Guard rules to carry life-saving fluorescent green dye, which could be spotted from the air in case a boat sank. Wouldn't you know, his dad had a pack of it sitting right there on the bench. Wouldn't you know, there was a fish pond in the middle of a circle driveway in front of Chippo's house. Wouldn't you know, one of us, I can't remember which one of us, got the bright idea of tossing the dye in the pond. We did it. It didn't take a rocket scientist to figure out where the dye came from. Any old doctor could do that. Anyway, Bobby got caught. To his credit, he never ratted on the rest of us, even though it cost him all the money he had saved for college and he had to scrub out the pond with rubber gloves and lye soap. It took him over a week to clean the pond and replace the flowers and goldfish that had died from the dye. Our swimming days at Chippo's were over. As it turned out, it didn't matter because that summer Lake Washington was closed to swimming because all those estates along the shore had been dumping raw sewage into the lake for so long, the lake had become totally polluted. It would be years before anyone would swim in it again.

Bobby did get his revenge, and I told his dad about it many years later on the occasion of my parents' 50th wedding anniversary. When I told him what Bobby had done to us, his dad broke into the best laugh I think he ever had. One of the other estates along the lake had some very large apple trees on it, a fence all the way around the property, and a large iron gate across the driveway. There was also something else on the property: two very large, very mean German Shepherds. One night Richard, Bobby and I were sleeping out in my backyard. About five in the morning we got a craving for apples. We climbed the nearest tree and were picking apples when Bobby started laughing out loud as he closed the gate. Richard and I looked down and stared into the eyes of the meanest dogs you ever saw. That was early in the morning. At dinnertime we could hear our mothers calling us, and the German Shepherds were still at the foot of the tree, just looking up at us. Bobby came and went all day long. He would stand outside the gate and laugh his head off. Finally the owner came home. He called his dogs off and asked us what we were doing up in his tree. He said, "If you wanted apples, all you had to do was ask." Our parents weren't so forgiving. They were just about to call the police when we got home. I think that was the second to last spanking I got from my father.

The last spanking I got came after our second foray into crime. One night Richard and I were again sleeping out. This time we got the great idea of stealing empty milk bottles off our neighbors' back porches and turning them in for the five-cent refund. I got my little red wagon, and we set out stealing empty milk bottles. By the time we got to the Red and White Grocery Store, my wagon was full. Mr. Reid, who owned the Red and White, didn't say a word. He just gave us 70 cents. Richard and I headed across the street to Mankey's Drug and loaded up on candy. Richard and I never slept out again after I got my last spanking. I guess today if a father spanks his kid, he can be hauled in for child abuse. All I can say is that for me it worked. I never stole anything again.

Like most every kid, I also have a Halloween story to tell. Our neighbor Jean Beal was my mother's best friend. We were about twelve years old. Really too old to be out trick-or-treating. Which of course we weren't. We were just up to "tricks." I guess just about everyone has heard of the dog doo in the paper bag trick. At the time it seemed like a good idea and very original. Well, we put some doo in a bag, placed it on Jean's front porch, soaked the bag with lighter fluid and were just about to light it when the front door burst open and Mrs. Beal, garden hose in hand, soaked us all to the skin. You don't know what cold and miserable are until you've been soaked to the skin on Halloween night in Seattle. I don't even remember what I tried to tell my parents. I guess it didn't make any difference since they already knew what had happened by the time we got home.

I spent my grade school years at Brighton Elementary on Holly Street. The school was about a mile and a half walk from our home, and it was the responsibility of the older kids to watch after the younger ones. We did have crossing guards and my last year at Brighton, I got to be one. For me it was a big deal. I got to yell at little kids and save them from being run over on Rainier Avenue. Actually, it was the first truly important responsibility I had ever been given, and I took it seriously.

My best subject in grade school was recess. I learned how to play with others and how to stay out of fights, for the most part. I had some really great teachers who took time to help me when I ran into difficulties. I started seeing girls in a different light although I had no idea what that meant. Just before the end of the school year, Brighton PTA held a carnival to raise money. One of the events was a "cake walk." You paid five cents and got into a circle that had one chair in the middle. When the music started, everyone started moving, and when the music stopped, whoever got to the chair and sat down first got a cake. I won five cakes that night. I learned a real good lesson that night when it became clear I could only carry one cake home.

The class ahead of us was the last class in the Seattle School District to receive eighth grade diplomas. I guess that was because all my classmates and I would be going to Sharples Junior High School on Graham Street for our eighth grade. The summer before Sharples, there were two tragedies for our classmates. In the first incident, one of a pair of twin brothers was killed in a gun accident. In the other incident, one of our classmates was in trouble with the law and jumped off a bridge, killing himself.

Sharples was a brand new school, and school as I knew it was really going to change. The biggest change would be girls and making new friends. My first new friend at Sharples was Jack Wylie. I also started running around with some guys from Columbia City, but that didn't last long. I stopped seeing them after they provoked a fight between me and a guy named Dennis. I broke Dennis's nose, and he and I were sent home to change clothes because his blood was all over both of us. By the time we got back to school, he and I had shaken hands and decided we had both been made into suckers. Dennis became a fireman and still lives in the area.

The only other important thing to happen to me at Sharples was meeting Beth.

I had seen her around school and really liked her. One day while walking home, I got up the courage, with the help of some friends, to ask for her phone number. That's the way it was done then. We didn't have cell phones or the Internet. I called her and we made a date to go to a movie. My heart sank when she told me that before we could go out, I would have to have dinner with her mother, father and brother. My mother had just bought me a suit for some family function, so when the day came I put on my suit and listened to my mother tell me how to act. I never heard a word she said. I took the Seward Park bus to Beth's house and was introduced to everyone. We sat down to a dinner of roast beef and mashed potatoes. Then the questions came. Mostly from her father. Who was my dad and what did he do? How was I doing in school? Did I have any brothers and sisters, and were any of them in trouble with the law? What did I think of Eisenhower and Truman? And on and on. Finally, I guess I must have passed because Beth and I were allowed to leave. We took a bus downtown and her father was to meet us at Rainier and Genesee at 9:30 p.m. When we got out of a movie, Beth had this great idea that we should go across the street and see another show. It was 11:30 p.m. when we got to Rainier and Genesee where her father was waiting, and that was the last time Beth and I went out. We did talk on the telephone one afternoon for four hours. My father had to have the operator interrupt our conversation and made me hang up. I saw her all the time at Franklin High School, but she was very popular and I can't remember if we ever talked again. I don't think so.

CHAPTER TWO: 1953 to 1957

In September 1953, I started at Franklin High School. Those were the very best of times for me and some of the worst of times. There were four things coming into my life that would change everything forever. Girls and cars, which both required money, and required the third change, work. Real work, not just mowing lawns and helping out around the neighborhood. The fourth change, as one might guess, was education. However it was not what I learned at Franklin that was important. It was what I didn't learn that led me to where I am today. To get to the first two changes I had to get a job. Luck was with me. One of my best buddies was Jim Garl. He was a year ahead of me, but his brother Danny was in my class. Danny had a job at a health food bar in downtown Seattle and was going to quit. With Danny's recommendation to become his replacement, I got the job. I was soon peeling carrots, washing potatoes and cleaning celery. That job was every day including Saturdays from 4:00 to 6:00 p.m, and the money was good. After that I landed a job at Luckers Meat Market, scrubbing butcher blocks and changing sawdust on the floor until about 7:30 p.m. every day, including Saturdays. I got three important things out of those jobs: great upper body strength, a car and money to blow on dates, which I did. There were dances on Saturday nights at the Mount Baker Club House, drive-in restaurants, drive-in movies, CYO dances, parties, lots of things to spend money on. Besides just the car. My first car was a 1953 Chevrolet. I wanted to buy a 52 MGB sports car, but my dad wouldn't let me. I loved my dad very much, but to be honest, I will never forgive him for not letting me buy what I really wanted. I know he was only thinking of my safety and what was best for me. But it was my money and I really wanted that car. The truth is, if my son or one of my daughters wanted to buy a similar car when they were sixteen, guess what I would have said, "NO."

In my freshman year, I signed up for drama and met a new girl who had transferred in from Oakland, California. Rhoda came into my life and was one of those changes that happen to just about every teenage boy. Boy, did I like Rhoda and I know she liked me. We dated for a little less than a year. Rhoda is Jewish and I knew that was a problem for some. But her mother and father treated me just great, and after a while I didn't think much about it. My mother suggested I invite her over for dinner. I thought that would be great. My mother served ham. A few days later Rhoda told me she had sent me a letter. In those days we got two mail deliveries a day, one in the morning and one in the afternoon. I skipped school and waited for the mailman. Her "Dear David" letter came in the afternoon. I was devastated. I don't remember everything in the letter, but I remember she thought I needed to find God.

That day there were torrential rains. I walked a few miles to the community park and found a cooking shelter where I sat and cried more tears than all the rain that fell that day. After that I started going to CYO (Catholic Youth Organization) with my friend from scouts, Jerry Banchero. That, however, didn't help much. Every time I would dance with a girl, she would ask which parish I attended and I would have to tell her I wasn't Catholic and that would end that. The one really good thing to come out this experience was that Jerry and I became very close lifelong friends.

All during this time my two closest buddies were Jack Wylie and Jim Garl, both a year ahead of me. They had joined a National Guard Unit to avoid the draft, so I convinced my parents to sign permission papers, lying about my age to let me join. You were supposed to be at least seventeen years old to join the Guard, and I was only sixteen. To this day my driver's license says I am a year older than I really am.

During my sophomore and junior years I did a lot of roller skating, dated different girls, hunted with my dad and brother-in-law Bob, and fished with my friend Jack Wylie. Jack and I would spend summer mornings down at Seward Park fishing by the hatchery. Now that I really liked, and I have been fishing ever since. I wasn't very good at hunting. My first year out I killed a doe. It took the heart right out of me. And yet, I had two chances after that to shoot a deer. One of those chances came while hunting with my friend Louie Patricelli. Lou was a year ahead of me and owned the Fabulous Drive-in on Rainier and I-90. Louie made the best hamburgers in town. Burgers were forty cents, fries were fifteen cents and a coke was a dime. We went there nearly every Friday night. One weekend Louie and I went hunting while his mother took over the shop. We were in Ellensburg, Washington, hunting deer, when out of nowhere there was this big buck, standing there just looking at me. I couldn't shoot, and he walked away. Luckily no one was around to see. When I got back to the cabin, Louie was making spaghetti and washing a bunch of mushrooms he had picked out in the woods. I asked him what he was doing, and he said he was going to put the mushrooms in the spaghetti. I asked him if that was safe and he said, "sure." Next, he put the mushrooms in a pan of boiling water, tied a dime to a string and tossed it into the pot. Again, I asked what he was doing. He said if the dime turned green, then the mushrooms were bad. If the dime came out bright silver, the mushrooms were safe to eat. The dime came out bright silver and I survived, so I guess he was right. But I'll never try that again.

I guess you could say this was a time when I was bouncing from pillar to post with no real direction. In the summer between my junior and senior years, the National Guard offered a six-month active duty program for its members. My friend Jack had graduated from Franklin and was going. I thought this was a good idea, so I went to Mr. Reseburg, Principal of Franklin, and we went over my transcripts. As it turned out, I only needed three credits to graduate. The six months were to start in August so I would be back in January or early February, which would give me time to earn three credits and graduate with my class. My parents signed the permission papers for the National Guard to send me, and I was off.

Jack and I traveled by train to El Paso, Texas and Fort Bliss. There must have been six hundred or more of us in transit and when we got to El Paso, we stepped off an air-conditioned train into one hundred degree plus weather. Guys were falling down all around me. But the Army was ready. They had ambulances and trucks to carry off those who couldn't walk. The rest of us were put on buses and taken out to our new quarters at Fort Bliss. Even though I would go on to spend ten years, five months and thirteen days of total military service, I was never really a very good soldier. I was always going outside without wearing my hat and forgetting to salute officers. I wasn't very good at the "sir" thing either. Someone always had to remind me about the hat, saluting and saying "sir."

There were two events that took place in basic training that have stayed with me all these years. The first happened when a young white soldier from Yakima, Washington got into a fight with a black soldier from somewhere in the south. The guy from Yakima was twice the size of the black guy and although I didn't see the fight, everyone said it was over real fast. I was on my bunk when the black guy came into the barracks, picked up an M1 rifle, went to his foot locker and took out some live rounds. I headed for the orderly room and told the officer in charge what I had seen.

He and I came around the corner of the barracks, and there was the black guy holding the M1 in front of him. Since I was the closest, I reached out to push him away. When I did he hit me in the face with the gun butt, knocking me to the ground. By this time others had arrived, and they took the gun away and held the black guy until the MP's arrived. He was later court marshaled and sentenced to six months in jail with dishonorable discharge. Nothing happened to the guy from Yakima or me. Well, almost nothing happened to me. I did get into a fight with one of the guys from the black guy's unit. He was white and it only took him one blow to break my nose. I don't know why but neither he nor I got in any trouble for that.

About six weeks into our training, we were on maneuvers out in the desert. We were on a break, sitting at the top of a steep ravine. When the order came for us to move out, I stood up and the world started spinning. I tumbled down into the ravine. I don't remember anything until I woke up on a table at Beaumont Army Hospital where doctors were pulling hair out of my leg. I spent several days there, but they could find nothing wrong with me, so I went back to my unit.

When our training ended, I returned to Franklin and was greeted by Ms. Olin, Attendance Secretary. She wanted to know where I had been; as far as she was concerned, I was truant and therefore automatically suspended from high school. I told her about Mr. Reseburg's permission for me to go on active duty for six months. That made her even more upset. In her mind, since I had been in the Army, I should not be allowed to be around young high school girls. I would also be a bad influence on the boys. She took her case all the way to the school board and before I could get back in, I had to agree to take my three credits between 7:45 and 10:15 a.m. and then be off the campus. That was okay with me because my brother Harry had gotten me a job at ABC Paramount Records in the stock room, which meant money, cars and girls.

It was about this time that a friend and I met Ilene and another girl downtown. I liked Ilene so I asked for her telephone number, which was the custom then, and she agreed to give me her number. She went to Ballard High School. When I asked her to a Valentine's Dance at the Mount Baker Field House, she accepted and I was to pick her up at 6:30 p.m. on a Friday night. When I arrived at her house, she greeted me at the door. She asked me to come in and meet her uncle. I was standing in her living room when out of the back comes this really big man, wearing a blue uniform with stars all over his shoulders. Ilene introduced her uncle who was Assistant Seattle Police Chief. He looked me over and asked me when I would have his niece home. I said, "midnight?" And he said, "I think 11:30 would be better." This time I remembered to say "sir" when I said, "yes sir." He looked me over again and said, "You know how I know you're going to have Ilene home by 11:30?" I said, "Yes sir, I think so." He said, "That's right. If you're not, every police car in the city will have your license plate right in front of them." Needless to say, Ilene was home by 10:30 p.m. and I never saw her again.

I met another girl, Myrna. She was one of the smartest girls I had ever met. Although I don't know what ever happened to her, she should have gone on to be a doctor, lawyer or professor, or something like that. She was just a naturally gifted academic. One day she and I were walking down the hallway at school when this guy comes up from behind and hits me in the back of the head. When I turned around, he hit me again. His name was Ron Santos. At the time I was five foot eight inches tall and weighed 139 pounds. Ron was over six feet tall and at least 180 pounds. We were to meet after school and finish the fight. There was no way I was going to do that. I was getting out of Dodge as fast as I could. I was at my locker getting my things together to leave when he and his entourage came up to me, and he apologized for hitting me. He later played ball for the Chicago Cubs and became a hall of famer. I had no idea why he hit me. It would be forty years before I would find out why he hit me. I was at a Franklin Hall of Fame induction for Ron when one of his friends told me I had done nothing to provoke Santos. He just liked to hit people.

I enjoyed my high school years, and I carry around a lot of pride in Franklin High School, not just because of my experience there, but because of what Franklin did for so many who came before me and so many who have come after. There is a certain pride you feel in Franklin whenever you come across a fellow alum, no matter when they graduated. Still, I must say that the most important lessons I should have learned in high school were not part of the curriculum. It's what I didn't learn in high school that was and is important. The good and the bad.

In addition to math and science, we had social studies, a euphemism for history. Some of the history handed down to us in class was either outright propaganda or at best half-truth. For example, when we studied World War II, we were told that the internment of Japanese Americans was for their own protection. We were not told that their homes and businesses were sold at sheriff auctions for non-payment of taxes. Americans were imprisoned solely because of their national origin, and while in prison they were unable to pay their property taxes so their property was lost. No textbook or teacher ever mentioned the 442nd Regimental Combat Team. The 442nd was an all Japanese-American combat infantry unit, mostly volunteers and some draftees, who served in Europe during the war. Theirs is the most decorated infantry unit in American military history. In one battle with an overwhelming German force, the 442nd suffered 800 combat casualties while saving 400 Texas Rangers who had been surrounded by the Germans. I think that would have been nice to know, especially for the Japanese-American students in our class.

We were taught about the Bataan Death March, which took place in the Philippines in 1942. The Japanese forces had captured 75,000 Filipino and U.S. soldiers. Those prisoners of war were force-marched 90 miles, during which approximately 650 Americans and 10,000 Filipinos died.

During my junior year we studied the opening of the west in American civics class. We learned about the Oregon Trail and the suffering of pioneers moving west to California, Washington and Oregon. We were never told that the United States government gave away land it did not own to pioneers willing to move west. Congress passed the Donation Land Claims Act in 1852, which gave 640 acres of land to each pioneer who would make the three-month trip west. That's one square mile per pioneer. All the while no treaties had been signed or titles ceded by the Indians to the United States government.

Another event in American history we were never told about was the Trail of Tears. In 1830 the Congress of the United States passed the Indian Removal Act, which resulted in the Cherokee, Creek and other tribes being forcibly removed from Georgia and surrounding states all the way to Oklahoma. Over 17,000 Native Americans were forced to march over 1,500 miles with over 4,000 of them dying along the way.

During our studies of WWII we were never told of the Tuskegee Airmen, African-American aviators who protected American bombers hitting Nazi targets deep inside Germany. The Tuskegee Airmen never lost a bomber to enemy fighter action, and they came home to segregation, hatred and bigotry, not to mention lynching by the KKK. In 2007 the last two hundred survivors of the Tuskegee Airmen received the Medal of Freedom from President George W. Bush. At the ceremony he said he would pay them tribute by offering them a salute from the Commander-in-Chief of all U.S. forces. At that point I thought *how dare* this draft-dodging National Guard deserter think he had the right to be in the same room with these heroes, let alone give them a military salute? Why do I feel so strongly about this? Because nothing could prepare me for what I saw when I arrived in El Paso, Texas. The segregated drinking fountains, bathrooms, restaurants, bars, buses and on and on. Not to mention, Bush has brought to an end all Federal Civil Rights enforcement activities. His politically appointed attorneys have told career civil servants that the Civil Rights Act of 1964 is unconstitutional and therefore will not be enforced, and he has purged hundreds if not thousands of African Americans from high level government positions during his term in office.

Should high school students be taught the true American history or should schools endeavor to produce good citizens by feeding them a watered down version of the American experience? That's a question seldom asked and yet to be answered. I for one believe that if a high school student is nearly eligible for the draft and the vote, then they need to be told the truth, good and bad, about our country. The truth will come out and make us stronger as a nation because of our diversity and unique ability to say we're sorry. Like we recently did to the remaining Japanese internees. Maybe some day our nation will muster the courage to say to African Americans that we're sorry for slavery and segregation. Maybe we can find it possible to say we're sorry for our policy of genocide against American Indians. Maybe some day.

—

Graduation day came and most of my class didn't even know I had returned to school. I had more people come up to me and say, "What are you doing here?" They didn't even know I had gotten back into school. I took Myrna to the Senior Prom and didn't see much of her after that. It seemed like all I did that summer and fall was go to weddings. I'm sure that 90% of the girls in my class got married that year. You must remember, this was before "the pill" and Planned Parenthood. One of the weddings was between my niece Linda and my best friend's brother, Danny Garl. They had four children, two girls and two boys. We don't see each other as often as we should, but we do care very much about each other and share some good memories. Linda's sister Barbara also got married at about the same time. It was a time before girls and young women had much of a chance at anything except becoming a wife and mother. The 1960's would change all of that.

In the summer of 1957, our National Guard Unit, the 770th AAA Battalion, went to summer camp at the Yakima Firing Range. AAA stands for Anti-Aircraft Artillery, and every year we would go to Yakima to fire the huge 120 mm guns. At the time this was state of the art for our national defense. We had a few black guys in our unit and they stayed pretty much to themselves. One guy in particular should never have been in the Guard. He was a little slow, to say the least. He was on guard duty one evening way out at the gun sit. Some of the white guys thought it would be a good idea to put on white sheets and go out and scare him. They did and after we got home, the black guy never came back to our weekend drills. After he had missed three weekend drills, Jim Garl and I were given MP badges, helmets and 45's. Of course we had no ammunition for these guns, but you couldn't tell just by looking. Our assignment was to get back all the military clothes and anything else owned by the Army that the guy had. We did as we'd been ordered. Several months later, during our formation at a weekend drill, our Company Commander informed us of what would happen if any of us were to miss three or more weekend drills. The black guy was sentenced to six months in jail and a dishonorable discharge. Nobody missed any drills after that, at least not that I know of. I sure know I didn't.

Other than that, everything was pretty uneventful that summer. I worked in a record company warehouse during the day and a Texaco gas station at night. My buddies and I would drive around chasing girls after I closed the station. If I had five dollars, I could gas up my car, pay for a movie and go to Gill's Drive-in for hamburgers, fries and a coke and still have money left over. A hamburger cost fifteen cents, fries were eleven cents, and a coke was a dime. That summer I met Autumn. Her family moved in behind our house on Myrtle Street.

CHAPTER THREE: 1958 to 1966

We turn around
We come around
We turn around
And what do we see?
We see what we want to see.

If there was ever a time in my life when I wish I could get a "do-over," this would be the time. A lot happened during these eight years. I went to Journalism and Public Relations School in Fort Slocum, New York, got married, had two children and endured six years on active duty in the Army. This was another period in my life when I just seemed to be going nowhere. I was looking for something to do with my life when the First Sergeant of our National Guard unit suggested I take a test for the U.S. Defense Department Journalism and Public Relations School in New Rochelle, New York. I would also need permission from our Company Commander, Captain Stryker. I took the test and did okay, and Captain Stryker thought it was a great idea to send me. By that time I was dating Autumn although none of my family or friends thought that was a good idea. They all encouraged me to go to New York, and they showed up at the train station to see me off. There must have been twenty people. Someone would have thought I was a potentate or something. I'm sure my mother arranged it all. Anyway, it sure felt good.

During the fifties, the Army was still shipping soldiers around the country by train. The trip from King Street Station in Seattle to Grand Central Station in New York was over 3,000 miles and took five days and four nights. I had a sleeper car and fell in love with train travel. Love it to this very day. When I arrived at Grand Central, I was to take a Greyhound Bus to New Rochelle. Not knowing where the bus station was, I hailed a cab. The cabby drove me all over New York. When we arrived at the bus station, I looked down the street two blocks and there was Grand Central. The cabby said, "That'll be twenty-five dollars." I pointed down the street to Grand Central and he replied, "one-way streets." I paid the twenty-five dollars and when I didn't give him a tip, he cussed me out as he drove off.

When I got to New Rochelle, I took a ferry to Fort Slocum. Fort Slocum was on David's Island. How appropriate. And what a beautiful place. With turn of the century red brick buildings, it looked just like a picture book of an eastern college. I followed the signs for new students to sign in and was greeted by a Sergeant who wanted to know who I was. It seemed I broke a rule by reporting in civilian clothes. I explained that our unit back in Seattle had not been issued the new Army green uniform. Next thing I knew, I was in the Commanding Officer's outer office, waiting to see him. When I was called in, of course I forgot to salute. He made me go back out and do it over again. This time I got it right. He said for me not to unpack because I would be going back on the next train. He told me to go to the orderly room and wait, which I did. In a little while I was called into the Company Commander's office and this time I remembered to salute properly. He told me to report to the Supply Sergeant's office to get fitted for new uniforms. I thought to myself, "I guess I'm in."

After getting my uniforms I was assigned to the third platoon. This was a Friday; on Monday morning I was called back to the Company Commander's office. This time he assigned me to the fourth platoon as platoon leader. The Sergeant who was the platoon leader had been in a car accident over the weekend and wouldn't be back. The Company Commander told me that since I was a Specialist Five and the only one he had, I was getting the job. I reported to the fourth platoon and called the men together. There were forty in all. I asked them how many were college graduates and about a third raised their hands. We still had a draft then and most of these guys who could have chosen to be officers decided two years as an enlisted man would be better than four years as an officer. I explained what had happened to the other Sergeant and passed on what the Company Commander had told me. Namely, we would be inspected every Saturday morning, and those platoons that passed inspection would be given weekend passes. Those who failed would spend the weekend cleaning their buildings and grounds. Almost all these guys were older than me and a whole lot smarter. I told them that if we were to get weekend passes, it would be up to them. One of the perks that came with being a platoon leader was a private room. I told them I would do my part by making sure my room passed inspection every time. Which I did. My mother would have been really surprised. Ours was the only platoon that passed its Saturday inspection every single time.

There was a nursing college in New Rochelle, and I met one of the nursing students. She wanted to take me into New York for dinner and a show. At the time you only had to be eighteen to drink in New York. We had a couple of drinks and dinner, during which time she asked me how big our ranch was, what my horse's name was and did we ever have any trouble with the Indians. There were those Indians again. I explained to her that we didn't have a ranch, the only horses I had were under the hood of a 53 Chevy, and we were surrounded by Italians, not Indians. I told her the place I grew up in was called "Garlic Gulch" and that it wasn't a reservation.

The school was great. Almost all of our professors were from neighboring colleges and very unmilitary. The journalism course was about ten weeks long and when it was over, I was really sad to be leaving. My brother Harry was working for a car dealer in San Francisco and had arranged for me to pick up a repossessed Plymouth and bring it to him. I found three guys who wanted to share expenses. I dropped one off in Saint Louis, one in Oklahoma City and the last one in Flagstaff, Arizona. The whole trip took 101 hours from New Rochelle to San Francisco, via Route 66. I had a little money from the Army so of course my brother had to sell me a car. Not just any car, but a new one with a balloon payment. I did drive it home to Seattle and got a job at Corey Sign Company for $25.00 per week plus commissions, and that's why the car went back to the dealer after about six months.

On July 4, 1959, Autumn and I were married in the same Presbyterian Church where I had attended Cub Scouts. I didn't like it any better being there the second time. Everyone was against this marriage. My friends, Jerry, Dale, Jack, Phil, Richard and Jimmy, everyone including all of my family members told me not to do it, to leave town instead. Go down to San Francisco and get a job with my brother, anything, just don't get married. Although Autumn told me she was pregnant, I later learned in fact she wasn't. It was a lie, but too late for me. I, of course, had to do the honorable thing and I did. For the next six or seven months, things went from bad to worse. Things were not going well selling signs. Autumn wouldn't work and jobs were hard to come by. We must have split up a half dozen times or more. I finally went to my old First Sergeant and asked to volunteer for active duty. I got to Fort Ord in March of 1960 and was waiting for reassignment when Autumn showed up with my brother Harry and his wife. Wouldn't you know it, I got assigned to the Fourth Infantry Division at Fort Lewis. There we were, right back home.

I was assigned to the Public Information Office at Fourth Infantry Division Headquarters. There I met a really great guy and friend, Captain Harry Hunke. Captain Hunke had been an eighteen-year-old corporal in the Philippines when the Japanese attacked. He was one of the survivors of the Bataan Death March. More than anyone else, he helped me adjust to military life, which for me was not easy. Autumn was continually causing trouble. I was being called down to the Company Commander's office almost on a weekly basis. They finally banned her from the post, so we moved into an apartment off base. My friend Jerry had just graduated from Santa Clara University where he had joined the ROTC and was now a Second Lieutenant in one of the Infantry units. He and Captain Hunke were about the only friends I had there.

Around November 1960 I received orders transferring me to a unit in Korea. I was to get thirty days' leave before reporting for shipment to Korea. I was on leave and staying at Autumn's parents' house when I got a call from Captain Hunke asking me if I would rather go to Canada than Korea. My response was an immediate, "of course." It seemed that while I was on leave, I came out on Department of Defense orders to Fort Churchill, Canada, and DOD orders get priority over Sixth Army orders. Since I had already been on leave for Korea, Captain Hunke had no obligation to tell me about the orders to Fort Churchill. Nevertheless, he did me a favor and let me know so I could decide where I wanted to go. What I didn't know yet was where Fort Churchill was. We got out a map of Canada and looked all along the border with the U.S. No Fort Churchill, that is, until someone looked up around northern Manitoba on the Hudson Bay and there was Fort Churchill, just inside the Canadian Arctic. Right at that moment Korea didn't look so bad, but it was too late. I had made my decision and I was stuck with it.

By the time I had to leave for Fort Churchill, Autumn and I had split up again. This time I had no intentions of ever going back with her. Fort Churchill was a one-year tour of duty, and no dependents were allowed. It was a Canadian Military Base located on the shores of Hudson Bay, said to be one of the coldest places on earth. The Army was still shipping people around by train, so I took the Northern Pacific to Fargo, North Dakota and transferred to a train going to Winnipeg. On the Winnipeg train I met a vice-president of the Canadian Pacific Railroad, and when we arrived in Winnipeg, he invited me to his house for dinner with his wife and family. His name was Woodward, and I had a very pleasant evening. I wrote to him and his family several times after I left the next day but eventually stopped and we lost contact. The train to Churchill was a narrow gauge railroad and after leaving Winnipeg, it never seemed to go faster than a person could walk. I later learned that because it was the middle of winter, the steel tracks were brittle and would break apart if they got too hot from the train wheels traveling over them. In fact when we got to Churchill, the train never stopped. They just kept it moving back and forth even as passengers were getting off and on.

When I stepped, or I should say jumped, off the train, I was in twenty degree below zero weather. In the brief time I was outside I felt like I was going to drop, like all those guys did when I arrived in El Paso. I reported in and was sent directly to the Supply Sergeant to be issued arctic gear. I was told never to go outside without wearing it. Most of the buildings were connected by enclosed, heated passageways. The Army used the base for winter testing of equipment. NASA had a testing site where they fired rockets into the atmosphere to measure radiation from Russian nuclear weapons testing in space. And the U.S. Air Force had a huge base where they were sending U-2 spy planes over Russia almost every day.

My job was to edit the base newspaper, the *Arctic Times*. This is where I learned about Army propaganda. While I was there, the Cuban Missile Crisis took place, but I was not allowed to mention it in the *Arctic Times*. I had to report on camp activities only; the rest of the news we got came from newspapers sent from home. The only radio station we could get was a Canadian Army station, and all they played was bagpipe music or Canadian country and western. No outside news reporting was allowed at all. I had my mother send me the *Seattle Times* and even though it arrived ten days to two weeks after the date of publication, it was very welcomed by everyone. After I finished reading the paper, it would make its way around the camp along with a few others that had been sent to other soldiers. The Canadians wouldn't let us fly the American flag outside, and I am sure our mail was censored or at least read.

I made some great friends at Fort Churchill: Paul Gouge, Willy Green and Captain Samples. While I considered Captain Samples a good friend, we didn't socialize. He was my supervisor and had been an enlisted man twice and an officer twice during his military career. We found a lot in common. We had many hours of what I consider great conversations. Paul, Willy and I palled around off duty. I always suspected that Willy was an undercover investigator, but he would never admit it. Although he had been in the same grade as Paul and I were, he was quite a bit older than us. He also seemed to know an awful lot about a Motor Sergeant being arrested for sending home tools from his motor pool and a Captain who was caught sending home a jeep. Of course the Sergeant went to jail and the Captain was allowed to resign his commission and go home. None of this could be reported in the *Arctic Times*, nor were we even supposed to talk about it.

Since outside activities were severely restricted, that left the base theater and the Sergeants' Mess, which included a full bar manned by a Canadian Army Corporal. Our dues were five dollars a month and paid for things like salt and pepper, salad dressing, catsup, mustard, etc. The Canadian Army did not provide those things to their mess halls. If you wanted them, you paid for them. The Sergeants' Mess was a very large place with a bar at least 30 feet long, a room with poker tables, and another room with pool tables and dartboards. As you may have guessed, I spent most of my off-duty hours there, mostly playing poker. I wasn't real good at it but I could hold my own. One weekend I started playing on Saturday afternoon and took breaks for dinner and then breakfast, lunch and dinner again. I was a few hundred dollars ahead when the game was over late Sunday night. I was really pleased with myself. There was a Master Sergeant in the game who came up to me afterward and shoved an envelope in my hand. He said, "Here, take this and put it in the bank for me on Monday. I'm leaving tonight and won't be back until late in the week." When I opened the envelope, I counted three thousand and forty one dollars inside. I kept the money under my pillow all night and never got a minute of sleep. I went to the bank as soon as it opened and deposited the Sergeant's money. I called in sick and slept the rest of the day. I played very little poker after that.

A day or two later I was walking up some stairs in our Headquarters Building when the room started to spin and I passed out, falling down a half flight to the first floor. I was taken to the hospital where a Canadian Army doctor examined me and decided I was malingering because he could find nothing wrong with me. I assured him I wasn't malingering, and he discharged me from the hospital. A month later, Paul, Willy and I jumped on the train with a load of groceries we got from the commissary and headed for a trapper's cabin at mile post 400. The two trappers who lived there were Emil and Harry, and they had a girlfriend named Sue. Paul had befriended them during the past summer and promised to bring them some supplies during the winter. They had no electricity, no running water, no radio, no TV, just a shortwave radio in case of emergency. You guessed it, they also had an outhouse. Try that in sixty-five below zero weather when all you have is a kerosene lantern and a roll of toilet paper. The remarkable thing about the trip was going to sleep that night; it was so quiet that I could actually hear my heartbeat. We went back down there in the summer and had three days of the most terrific fishing I had ever had. We caught northern pike, trout and graylings. Before leaving we asked Harry what we could bring them, and he said as much toilet paper as we could carry. We did.

About six months into my tour, the Army changed the rules that allow spouses in the camp. The next thing I knew, Autumn was on the way up. I don't know how she found out about the change in Army policy or how she managed to get permission to join me but she did. Just before she arrived, I was doing a story about a helicopter unit stationed there when a Royal Canadian Police helicopter arrived with two baby polar bears aboard. I got to carry one of them into a building where they were going to try to save them. The one I carried was a little ball of energy and fit into the palm of my hand. The cubs died a few days later. Polar bears around there were as common as robins in the spring.

Everyone stationed at Fort Churchill had to spend three days on an Arctic survival course. When it was my turn, I was assigned to a six-member team. We were given an eight-foot sled to carry our supplies, food and a large tent. They put us on a helicopter and dropped us out in the wilderness. We had to find our way back to camp. Since we could not see any horizon, we had to rely on a compass to find the right direction. If we were wrong, we were screwed. Someone would have to come and find us, and that would not be good. We were all issued machetes, for what I couldn't imagine. As it turned out we used them to cut ice blocks to put around our tent on the first night out. The blocks helped keep the wind from blowing our tent away. On the second night out we found ourselves at the edge of the Air Force runway. We were supposed to dig an ice cave in the bank and spend the night, getting up the next morning and walking back into camp. We were also right next to a tank testing area. I went out and flagged down a passing M-60 tank, climbed into the turret, unrolled my sleeping bag and slept there all night while the tank drove back and forth on its test run. It was like riding on a Greyhound Bus with steel seats. But it was warm and a lot more comfortable than sleeping in an ice cave. Through all this I learned just how cold a human being could get and still live. I never want to be that cold again.

Autumn arrived. Everything went downhill after that. People who had been my friends wouldn't talk to me anymore. Paul and Willy stood by me though, and I will always appreciate them for that. They actually made it possible to get through it all.

I had been in Churchill about thirteen months, Autumn about four months, when we got news that the Army was getting out and moving to Alaska for their winter testing. Orders came down for me to be stationed at Fitzsimmons Army Hospital in Aurora, Colorado. We cleared quarters and so did Paul and Willy, and our First Sergeant Sanders held a party for us. I don't know why, but Sergeant Sanders told me that Autumn had cost me a promotion to Staff Sergeant. He didn't say how she did it, just that she did. It was becoming clear to me once again that I had to get out of the relationship.

After a short leave at home, I reported in to Fitzsimmons and was assigned to the Hospital Public Relations Unit. For the next year all I did was conduct tours of the hospital and other military facilities around the area. On January 10, 1963, Candie Lynn was born. In the summer of 1963 we took a vacation back to Washington so everyone could see Candie. While we were there, I took time to go out to Fort Lewis and see some of my old friends. I told Captain Hunke that I was bored to death at Fitzsimmons and was looking for a new assignment. When I got back to Fitzsimmons, I was informed that I had come out on order assigning me to a Sixth Army Headquarter Unit at Fort Lewis, Washington. I asked Captain Hunke on several occasions if he had anything to do with my orders, but he would never answer.

We were assigned base housing, and I reported to the Public Relations Office where I was once again working for Captain Hunke. This office had a radio station and Information Specialists who wrote Army news stories for the local media and individual home town newspapers, stories about promotions, awards to returning Vietnam veterans, things like that. There was also a newspaper called *The Fort Lewis Ranger.* The publisher of the paper was a Journalism professor from University of Washington. He had held the contract for publishing the *Ranger* for many years, but there was a conflict with the local newspaper, *The Lakewood Press*, which wanted to take over the contract for the *Ranger.*

Under the contract with the professor, a soldier would be assigned as editor of the *Ranger* and a civilian would be hired to sell advertising. Shortly after I arrived, the editor at the time was reassigned and I was asked if I would take his place. When I took the offer, I didn't know that the publisher paid the editor $300.00 and the sports editor $250.00 under the table. The reason for these payments was that both jobs required several hours a week in overtime work and trips to Olympia where the paper was printed. Several of the Officers in the office didn't like this arrangement and were constantly asking us how much we were being paid. Somehow they found out and the next thing I knew, the contract was going to the Lakewood Publishers and I was reassigned to the U.S. Army Recruiting Station in Seattle as their Public Relations Specialist.

We found housing in Seattle in Mount Baker near where I had grown up and gone to high school. I had a little over a year of service on my enlistment and often have thought either God or Captain Hunke was looking after me since I could have just as easily been sent to Vietnam to finish my career. Autumn was carrying our son David Jr., who was born on June 23, 1965. As usual she had alienated everyone in the neighborhood and people I had to work with in very short order.

By this time I had made up my mind to divorce her as soon as I could get out of the Army. I had decided to get out long before this assignment in Seattle, but I knew I had to wait because the Army didn't like divorces and would force us into counseling for a long time. I also wanted out because I was completely against the war in Vietnam by this time. I knew we were wrong to be there, and I sure didn't want to go.

There were some really good people at the Recruiting Headquarters: Sergeant Major Wiggins and Colonel Travis. Travis was a direct descendent of the Alamo Travis and had graduated from West Point in 1941. Sergeant Major Wiggins seemed to understand my problems with Autumn and would run interference for me when she would call him making trouble for me. There was also a First Lieutenant there who was a little squirrelly. We had a deal with the two local newspapers; we had agreed that we would not call both of them for the same story. There was also an Army Colonel named Bond and his son, James Bond, who was enlisting and just happened to have a serial number with 007 in it. The First Lieutenant insisted that I call both papers to cover the story. After reminding him of our agreement with the two daily papers, I did as he had ordered. As a result neither paper would cover any of our events for the next several months and after that only on condition that they be given an exclusive story.

The Lieutenant later volunteered to go to Vietnam so he could earn a Combat Infantry Badge or CIB. At the time the only way someone could get this badge was to spend 30 days in combat with an enemy. I thought he was crazy. It is one thing to be ordered into combat and a whole other thing to volunteer. He went to Vietnam and returned wearing a CIB. He said it was good for his career.

During the 60's there was still a draft, and a lot of young men were signing up to avoid the draft; to this day I don't really understand the logic in that. But recruiters were telling young men that if they enlisted, they would avoid the draft and be able to pick a school that would keep them out of the infantry and out of Vietnam. If they enlisted, they would be able to pick from three different schools for training. For example, they could pick helicopter mechanic as a first choice and if they didn't get that, they could pick their second choice, say bakery school, and if not that they could pick their third choice, say intelligence school. What the recruiters didn't tell the suckers was that their chances of getting into any of these schools was next to none. In our recruiting district alone we would make these kinds of deals with hundreds of recruits every month when in fact there were only one or two openings per month among the schools offered by the Army. The catch was, there was another "promise" in the enlistment documents signed by recruits: "Assignments will be made at the convenience of the Army," which in most cases meant infantry and Vietnam. I don't think much has changed now, even with an all-volunteer Army, except that now they are recruiting men and women in other countries and in our nation's prisons.

I didn't mind working at the recruiting station because I was coasting to my enlistment date and about to get out. Early in March I went to get out of bed in the morning and fell over, the room spinning like a top. I couldn't stand, speak or move a muscle. Autumn called for help, and an ambulance came and picked me up and took me to Fort Lawton Army Hospital, which was still operating at the time. By the time we got to the hospital, I was coming out of whatever had happened to me. There were two doctors who saw me. One was a civilian doctor and her opinion was the same as the Canadian Doctor, that I was faking it. The other doctor was an Army doctor named Snyder. He wanted to keep me for some further tests, so I was at Fort Lawton for the next two weeks. Captain Snyder called me in and said he thought he had found out what was wrong with me. His diagnosis was Meniere's Syndrome, an inner ear problem causing dizziness and seasick-like symptoms. The next day he sent me to Madigan Army Hospital near Fort Lewis for confirming tests. It was as he thought. One thing that has always confused me was being called into a Colonel's office where he gave me the news that I did in fact have Meniere's but that given the circumstances, he was not going to give me a medical discharge. I never did know what the "circumstances" were, nor did I care. I had less than a month left in the Army.

When I got back to Fort Lawton Hospital and told Captain Snyder what the Colonel had said to me, Snyder said not to worry, that he would take care of it. A few days later he called me into his office and said he was discharging me on medical leave until my enlistment was up. He also instructed me about what to write on my documents prior to discharge. I went home and checked in with the recruiting station. They were surprised to hear from me since they thought I had gone AWOL. No one, including Autumn, had told them where I was. I was ordered to report immediately.

When I arrived, the Lieutenant now Captain threatened to have me court marshaled. Sergeant Major Wiggins came to my rescue and pointed out that I was not AWOL since I was in an Army hospital and carried on their morning report. It was an Army mistake that the hospital didn't notify them where I was.

A day later our Company Clerk Rutherford came and told me I had been promoted to Staff Sergeant and I would be called into the Company Commander's office anytime now to get my new stripes. Several days later the Captain and Sergeant Major Wiggins were coming down the hall, so I stopped the Sergeant Major to ask him about my promotion. The Captain interrupted and said he was not going to promote anyone who was not staying in the Army. As usual I did a dumb thing. I said, "I wasn't aware that promotions were based on future intent rather than past performance." It was all Wiggins could do to keep that Captain off of me. He wanted my butt in the worst way. Wiggins sent me home until it was time to go to Fort Lewis for mustering out.

There was one last hassle with the Army before I got out. My friend Jerry Banchero had been selling some Amway shoe polish that made your shoes really shine and I had been using it. The only thing was, after a while the shoe leather would crack and peel. I reported to Fort Lewis wearing my cracked and peeling shoes. Again, I was taken to task. The Sergeant in charge of the separation station took me aside and asked what it was I had on my feet because they surely were not Army shoes. I told him the story and said I would be happy to go and buy some new Army shoes, which I would only wear once, to my home. He asked me where I lived, so I told him Seattle. Once he confirmed that I would not be flying or taking the train, that I had my car there, he let me go. And that ended my Army career. In September of 1966 when I was a civilian again, I received a letter from the Veterans Administration awarding me a thirty percent Service Connected Disability, retroactive to my discharge date, April 9, 1966.

We rented another house on Beacon Hill, and I got a job selling printing for Trojan Lithograph in Renton. It wasn't long before I had moved out from Autumn and the kids. In today's world I probably could have kept the kids but not at that time. Fathers had no legal rights except the requirement to pay child support. My friend Jack had an extra room so I moved in with him.

It took about six months before the divorce was final. I had to pay child support and was to have the children every other weekend. Autumn would never let me see both kids at the same time. I got either Candie or David but never both. I was told there was nothing the courts could do about that. I went to pick up the kids one weekend, but Autumn and the kids were gone. The only thing my mother could find out from Autumn's relatives was that they had left the state. I wouldn't see Candie again until she was 18 years old and running from the law in Las Vegas. I finally caught up with David Jr. when he was 19 years old and in the Air Force.

CHAPTER FOUR: 1967 to 1972

Having Candie and David taken away from me has hurt me more than anything else in my life has, even to this very day. Candie is lost in drugs, and I have yet to find a way to reach her. My son David and I have come together, and I am very, very proud of the life he has made for himself and his family. Nonetheless, I feel as though I somehow let both of them down by not trying harder to find them when they were still little kids. Had I done that, maybe things would have worked out differently for Candie. I guess I'll never know and should be grateful that things have worked out so well for David and his family.

As sad as I was when I found my children had been taken away from me, I was at the same time feeling, "FREE AT LAST, FREE AT LAST." Autumn was out of my life. At the time I was working for Trojan Lithograph and MALMANCO Printing Company in Renton, Washington. I was living with my friend Jack and earning $150.00 a week plus commissions. I got the job at Trojan because they were one of my dad's customers. Come to think of it, at least two of the three jobs I had before and after the Army were because of my dad. Besides the $150.00 per week, Trojan paid all my health insurance and I paid $17.00 a month to cover Autumn and the two kids, not that it ever got used. Today, few if any employers pay any health benefits and if they do, the employees pay the biggest share for themselves and their families. We have Reagan to thank for the wholesale destruction of our nation's health care system.

It was during a Christmas Party for Trojan and MALANCO that I met Carol Proctor. She was a technical illustrator at MALANCO, and we started dating shortly after the holidays. Carol had graduated from the University of Washington with a degree in Interior Design and had been working at MALANCO for a couple of years. We got along fine although I could tell her mother Kay and father Gerald didn't like me at all. They lived on Mercer Island; Kay was a very successful real estate agent and Gerald was an executive with Bell Telephone. I think they thought Carol could do much better than me. I think they would have preferred a doctor or lawyer or even a dentist over me. Anyone would be better than a divorced printing salesmen. Plus, I don't think they liked my politics or lack of religious convictions.

These were very exciting times; the whole world was upside down with the war in Vietnam and the War on Poverty going on at the same time. I saw these days as a great hope for a better America. Carol's whole family was very conservative, to say the very least. I, on the other hand, was a flaming, bleeding heart liberal, maybe even a little radical at the time. I did take part in demonstrations for civil rights and against the war. 1967 - 1968 was a particularly volatile time in American history, with Kent State and the assassinations of Bobby Kennedy and Martin Luther King, whom were both characterized by Kay and Gerald as communist tools just as the anti-war movement was seen as absolutely un-American.

Carol and I got married on December 23, 1967. We were married by Judge Love of Bellevue Municipal Court. Carol's parents refused to attend, so I asked my parents not to come. After the ceremony Carol's father took everyone including my parents to the Golden Lion Inn at the Olympic Hotel and held a dinner for us. At the time, and still to this day, I thought that was really big of him. Our daughter Kristin Heidi was born on February 12, 1968. What a treasure she has turned out to be.

About this time an old Army friend asked me to be Director of Public Relations for the 1968 Armed Forces Spectacular to be held at the Seattle Center. I know it seems a little odd for me to accept this position, given my feelings against the war. However, I wasn't against the soldiers, sailors and airmen fighting the war, just against those who caused it to happen to begin with. Another big factor in taking the job was all the printing work I could bring to Trojan. At the time my nephew, Dr. Calvin Winslow Jr., my sister Jane's oldest son, was head of the Socialist Workers Party in the State of Washington and running as Eldridge Clever's Vice Presidential Candidate on the Peace and Freedom ticket.

It seemed that at this time no one was happy with me. Carol's family hated my politics, and my sister and others in my family couldn't understand how I could be such a hypocrite. Now I think they both had a point. But at the time it all made sense to me. The most interesting thing about the whole experience was the day the big show opened and nobody showed up.

It was a completely empty center. I thought they would call off the next day's show, but they didn't. The show must go on, and sure enough, no one showed up for the second performance, not even one of the patriots in Carol's family. The one good thing was that my boss at Trojan was happy about the work I brought in.

During the summer of 1967, I played the part of Billy the Kid in a documentary filmed by Bob Allen who also worked at Trojan as an illustrator. We went on location during the weekends in various places around Seattle and in Eastern Washington. I got the part because Bob had me dress me up as Billy the Kid, and he took pictures that he later turned into tin-type and sure enough, I looked just like the famous outlaw. The documentary was narrated so I didn't have any speaking parts, but it was great fun anyway and the film won an award at the San Francisco Film Festival that same year.

Also during that summer another employee of Trojan Lithograph, Gene Palm, and I went into business with Trojan Lithographic and opened Auburn Quick Copy in Auburn, Washington. We had hoped to get some contracts with the Boeing Company through MALMANCO, which did not happen, and the result was there was not enough income to support the both of us. I volunteered to leave the business to Paul.

Jobs were hard to find around Seattle at the time, so I took a job in Palo Alto, California managing a Crosby Paint Store. Carol stayed with her parents until I could find us a place to live. On the way down there I stopped in San Francisco to see my brother Harry. He had a friend named Tom Moore whose girlfriend owned a photography studio in Union Square. She had sent out coupons for free pictures, and Eldridge Clever had sent one in. At the time Eldridge Clever was the head of the Black Panthers Party in San Francisco. My brother and Tom dared me to deliver the award for a free picture to the Black Panthers Headquarters just a few blocks away. I took them up on the dare and walked to the headquarters. There were two big black guys at the door who asked me what I wanted, so I explained. They called upstairs and the door was buzzed open for me.

I climbed the stairs and was greeted by Angela Davis. I told her why I was there and also told her I was Calvin Winslow's uncle. We had a great conversation, and she has since become one of my heroes because of her years of work on prison reform. I told my brother and Tom what had happened, but they didn't believe me until I showed them the signed coupon for a free photograph. In the "land of the free and home of the brave," our prisons hold one hundred black males for every one black male in college. My brother and Tom, like millions of others, feared people like the Black Panthers and Angela Davis, and never bothered to consider their struggle.

I continued on to Palo Alto, found a house to rent and started my job at Crosby Paint. It wasn't long before I discovered why I had the job title of Manager even though I was the only one working in the store. Managers can't join a union. Carol and Kristin soon joined me, and Cary was born at Stanford University Hospital on January 13, 1969. I really didn't like being tied down to the store and was looking to find a better job when one morning about 6:00 a.m. I couldn't sleep and went down to the store. When I got there, I found the door unlocked and a guy in the back room. Crosby had a policy of making deposits of the day's receipts everyday, holding back $100.00 in bills and change for the next day. I was required to put the money in an empty paint can and put it on a shelf in the back room. The guy in the store had the paint can in his hands and was putting money in it. I was ready to call the cops when he identified himself as a detective hired by Crosby to see if I would take any money over the $100.00 that was supposed to be in the can. I called my supervisor and told him I needed to see him right away, as soon as he could get there. He arrived and I made him count the money in the cash register and handed him the keys to the store. I told him I wouldn't work for anyone who didn't trust me, so "he could take this job and shove it."

Within a few days I had landed another job, this time more to my liking, as a salesman for a printing shop in Mountain View. I got a company car and $150.00 per week plus benefits and commissions. About two months into the job, my boss called me in and told me he had to let me go. His nephew was out of work and needed a job, and he couldn't afford two salesmen. He was going to give me two weeks severance pay, but he couldn't afford to pay me the $5,000.00 commission I had earned from a very large job I had brought in. He said he was giving that account to his nephew. As anyone can imagine, I was pretty pissed off by the time I got home. Things were not going well at all. Carol was very understanding, and we spent a few days weighing our options. One of the things I had been considering for a long time was going back to school. We decided we would go back to Seattle and look into the possibility of using my GI Bill to cover tuition.

When we got back, we lived with her parents while I considered various possibilities. A new community college had opened in Auburn, Washington, Green River Community College, so I went there to talk to an enrollment counselor. I decided to take the SAT and see how well I could do. The day came and I walked into a room full of newly graduated high school students. I really got scared, here I was 30 years old and going up against newly minted high school graduates. As it turned out, I had nothing to fear as I did rather well on the SAT and started the GI Bill and student loan application process soon after that.

Carol, the girls and I needed a place to live. As it turned out, Sea Port Development was building some low-income housing across the street from Green River called Lea Hills. The housing units were an experiment by King County and the U.S. Department of Housing and Urban Development. The Regional Director of HUD was a guy named Andy Hess; he was a good friend of my sister Janie. The idea was for a contractor to get building code breaks in order to build more affordable housing. Some parts of the house had common walls, and various codes were waived to cut costs. Carol's mother helped us buy our first house by giving us her commission, which we used as a down payment on a two-bedroom, one-bath house for $16,000.00. The complex had 52 houses, a clubhouse with a swimming pool and a recreation room. Things were really looking up. I started school and met Robert Johnson who would become one of my very best friends. Robert is Hispanic and would later change his name to Robert Franco, which was his father's name.

It was around this time when I started to notice some strange behavior from Carol. I asked her mother if she knew of anything wrong with Carol, and she told me Carol had been diagnosed with schizophrenia. I asked her why she hadn't told me this before, and she said she thought I already knew. I got Carol's doctor's name and went to see him. He explained her condition and told me it would only get worse as she got older but that her condition could be managed if we could keep her on her medication, which as it turned out, was almost impossible to do.

Carol had made a decision early on that she was going to stay home and take care of the girls, and I agreed. She was a terrific mother. The girls always had something to do. She filled their days playing in the yard, doing art projects, taking them to the zoo and other kids' activities. Our house was always the center for neighborhood kids.

Classes started in September 1969. By then we were all moved into our new house. I got the GI Bill, which amounted to about $300.00 a month. That covered books and tuition. I also received financial aid and got a job driving the afternoon school bus for the Auburn School District. Between all three sources of income, we were doing pretty well. I was really nervous on the first day of school, still worried about competing with kids right out of high school. After all I was 30 years old.

At the suggestion of a friend, I had filed a claim with the California State Attorney General against my former employer for the $5,000.00 commission before I left for home. We had just moved into our new home when I received a check for $4,700.00. My former employer had been ordered to pay the commission, so he had deducted the two weeks of severance pay he had given me, which was okay with me. Things really were looking good.

One of my first instructors was Professor Nigel Adams. He taught history and social science. We hit it off and he soon became my advisor. I also took a couple of journalism classes and soon became bored with that since I knew as much or more than the professor teaching it. I thought about teaching as a career, but Dr. Adams suggested that I wouldn't make it as a teacher for more than a year. Either the school administration or the parents would run me off for what I would be teaching young high school students. Now that I look back on his advice, I can see how wise he was. I wasn't devious enough for political science or smart enough for any of the social sciences, hard sciences, math or English, so that pretty much left history, which for me was a great choice.

As it turns out every discipline requires specific writing styles and methods. For example, in journalism you learn to determine the facts of a story and arrange them with the most important facts first, providing more detail as the story unfolds. In history, however, you start with an investigation of an event and collect facts until you reach a conclusion about what those facts mean. Every attorney I've worked with has liked my investigative reports because they're short and to the point. I could do a report or letter of findings in three to five pages; other investigators would take twenty pages to accomplish the same thing.

There was an active Veterans Against the War group at Green River; Robert, another Lea Hills owner, and veteran Don Evans, and I all participated in demonstrations and other activities. All three of us were also on the Lea Hills Board of Directors. One of the things the veterans didn't like about Green River's graduation requirements was having to take three credits of physical education, which meant running around the track everyday. They saw it as very "high school." I didn't have to take it because I was a disabled vet. However, I agreed to help other veterans get rid of or change the requirements. As one Vietnam Vet said, "I've carried a sixty pound pack, MC 16 rifle, ammunition, had people shooting at me for weeks on end, and now you want me to run around a track in my shorts with a bunch of little kids." We got the requirements changed, allowing students to participate in any college activity like student government, school newspaper or music programs to get the activities credit. The physical education instructor was not happy with me, and after a rather heated meeting he had the entire basketball team surround me, back me up against a wall and threaten to beat me to a pulp if I didn't leave their program alone. Dr. Adams and another professor came to my rescue. The next morning I went into the Dean of Instruction's office and unloaded on him for allowing what happened to happen. Needless to say, I was thrown out of his office by security. We never spoke again.

While all that stuff was going on at school, stuff was going on at Lea Hills as well. Most of the units had sold by April or May 1970, and owners were beginning to encounter construction problems, such as framing that was not bolted to the concrete slab, ivy growing up under the frame and up the walls, property lines running down the middle of living rooms, water spigots on someone else's property, leaking roofs, and mold and mildew in the clubhouse so extensive that the King County Health Department wouldn't allow us to use it until it was fixed. We contacted Sea Port Development, but they refused to do anything about it. They said our homeowners' dues and special assessments were to be used to fix any problems.

At this point the homeowners voted to get an attorney. Robert, Don and I were selected to find an attorney and do something about these problems. We went to see Alva Long. We picked him because he had taken on the state's Blue Laws and won. The Blue Laws said that nothing could be sold on Sundays in Washington State. However, the state determined that only beer, wine and hard liquor would be subject to the Blue Laws. Alva would go into a drug store on Sundays to buy some shaving cream or toothpaste, pay for his purchase and then call the police to have the manager and clerk arrested for Blue Law violations. After a few of these episodes, the state stopped enforcing the Blue Laws at least as far as beer and wine were concerned. We thought this was our man. All three of us went to his office on a Saturday morning. That was the only time he would see prospective clients. We waited in his outer office and were finally called in. All four of his office walls were covered with law books, and there was no furniture except the high stool he sat on next to his desk. He told us later that there were no chairs because he didn't want anyone settling in. He just wanted to hear the problem, think about it and get back to the client as to whether or not he was going to take the case. That's what he did with us, and in a few days he called to say he would take our case pro bono.

Alva conducted an investigation and found that while King County and City of Auburn had granted some building code waivers, they had not authorized the use of substandard materials or deviations from blueprints and building plans. They found that in places that called for three-quarter inch treated plywood, the builder had used untreated quarter-inch plywood. In places that required copper piping, they had used plastic instead. In other words, they had gone way beyond what was intended when some building codes were relaxed to build affordable housing. After several meetings with the homeowners association and Alva, we came to admire and appreciate what he was doing for us. He once told us that his dad had been a juvenile court judge and wanted him to be a lawyer but he wanted to be a bum, so they compromised and he became a bum lawyer. He was anything but. He filed suit against Sea Port, HUD, King County and City of Auburn. He also advised us to open a trust account and deposit our mortgage payments there until the matter was resolved. We got a lot of press and soon we were offered a settlement. We could keep our mortgage payments, our mortgages would be dissolved with no adverse credit reporting, and we would have our pick of any HUD repossessed home. All this took place just as I was getting ready to transfer to Western Washington University in Bellingham.

Nigel had introduced me to Professor Delorum at Western's history department. I had applied and was accepted. On a trip to the campus, I learned about the College of Ethnic Studies and decided to check it out. There I met Sioux Indian attorney and author Vine Deloria Jr., and my life took another dramatic turn. Here's that Indian thing again. The College of Ethnic Studies and Vine presented me with a whole new outlook on history, life and the world we live in. For example, I never knew why Custer was called "Son of the Morning Star." It was because he developed a strategy of attacking Indian winter camps at first light and killing men, women and children as they came out of their lodges; then his men would burn down the entire camp. I never knew that the Japanese attacked us at Pearl Harbor because they thought we were going to cut off their supply line for coal and oil from Southeast Asia. I never knew that it was the intent of President Taylor to annex most of northern Mexico down to Baja for a deep water shipping port, only to be thwarted by Secretary of State Stockton who signed a treaty placing the borders where they are today. I didn't know just how bad slavery really was or how it came about or the terrible things that happened to African Americans during the many, many years of segregation. I never knew that Japanese Americans lost all their property due to internment.

Needless to say, the rest of the University didn't like the idea of an Ethnic Studies College right in their midst. It didn't help when Dr. Will Wasson, the first Native American from Oregon to earn a PhD, offered a class called "Native American Culture: Everything You Wanted to Know but Were Afraid to Ask." Classes began Monday morning, and the room was filled with political science, anthropology, history, social science and education students. There were also several of us from ethnic studies. Dr. Wasson walked into the class, counted the students and sat down behind a table. He waited a while, then took out a newspaper and began to read. As the class hour was coming to a close, students began to leave. The next day, the same thing only with fewer students in the class. Dr. Wasson counted, sat down, took out a book and began to read. As the hour ended, more students started walking out. The next day, the same thing, only this time a student raised his hand and Dr. Wasson recognized him. The student said, "Dr. Wasson, are you going to teach anything?" Dr. Wasson said, "Sure. What do you want to know?" He went on to explain that in his culture it was impolite to offer opinions or facts without first being asked. He went on to point out that his class was subtitled, "Everything You Wanted to Know about Indians but Were Afraid to Ask." Meanwhile the students who had left the class went to the Dean of Instruction and filed a formal complaint against Dr. Wasson for not teaching his class. We all came to Dr. Wasson's defense, and the complaint was dropped.

The College of Ethnic Studies came about as a result of African-American students and the University of San Francisco strike to get a black studies program. The departments of political science, education, anthropology and social science all wanted ethnic studies gone. The only friends we had were some individuals in the history department. The opponents to ethnic studies finally got their way in 1972 when a Hispanic dean was hired; he was completely out of his mind. He single handedly took down the College of Ethnic Studies by alienating everyone on campus. It was the first time I had encountered this tactic to get rid of something the establishment didn't want, but it wouldn't be the last. I graduated in September 1972 and started looking for a job.

PEACE AND TRANQUILITY

Give me peace and tranquility
I've fought my battles
I've fought my wars

I picked up a gun when I was young
Carried it over shiny buttons

I put the gun down
Fought anew for peace with dignity
I manned the barricades
Bare hands and voice raised

I shouted angry words
After the war
After the barricades were gone
I kept up the roar for the hungry, homeless and sick

It's time for others to roar
My voice is sore
I need peace and tranquility
And not much more

CHAPTER FIVE: 1973 to 1980

Carol and the girls lived with me in student housing during my first quarter at Western. Carol didn't like it there, so she and the girls took an apartment in Kent next to Robert's wife and kids, and he and I rented an apartment in Bellingham. We spent the weekends at home with our families and the weekdays in Bellingham. I will always be grateful that Carol was so understanding and supportive of my decision to go back to school. I don't think I could have done it otherwise.

The most important thing I learned in school was that each discipline has its own language and problem-solving methods. Doctors, lawyers, engineers, social scientists and ethnic studies scholars all have different ways of communicating and analyzing problems. While it is true that no one can truly understand discrimination emotionally unless he or she has been a firsthand recipient, one can understand discrimination academically through study and the learning process.

And you do not have to be a recipient of discrimination to recognize it when you see it. Those segregated drinking fountains and bathrooms I saw in El Paso were real and I knew full well what they meant. What ethnic studies offered me was an appreciation of what others have been through and an understanding of the language and thought processes being used in everyday problem solving by minorities, women and disabled people. Ask most anyone what discrimination is and they will say, it's when white people treat people of color unfairly. While that's true, discrimination goes far deeper than that; discrimination is an unfair or demeaning act committed by anyone against anyone else based on race, color, national origin, sex or handicapping condition. And yes, white people can be discriminated against if the unfair or demeaning act committed against them is based on race, color, national origin, sex or handicapping condition.

Also, many people today will tell you that discrimination no longer exists in our society because of laws passed in the 1960's and 70's. The truth is that discrimination has not gone away; it's just that individuals, businesses and governments have become better at hiding it. Since Reagan, civil rights compliance and enforcement have been abandoned. One civil rights attorney in the Bush administration instructed the U.S. Department of Commerce, Economic Development Administration and Civil Rights Department to stop all compliance activity because the 1964 Civil Rights Act was unconstitutional.

Jobs were few and far between when I graduated from Western. I was getting discouraged after about five months of not finding anything I wanted to do. Then the right job turned up although Carol didn't think I should take it because there was no money in the budget for my salary. The job was as Director of the South King County Multi-Service Center in Federal Way. The Office of Economic Opportunity (OEO), one of President Johnson's War on Poverty programs, had pulled all the funding from the program because of mismanagement on the part of the previous Director. I saw the job as a challenge. I took it on and got the funding back and the padlock off the door. Within a few weeks we had family counseling services back, a senior citizen transportation program, a food bank and a job placement program, all operating out of a new building for the center.

One of the ladies working in the seniors program was Francis Kirk, and she was just terrific. Everybody loved her. I happened to mention one day that I needed bean poles for my garden, and Francis said she had a whole backyard full of bean poles. She invited me to her house in Black Diamond to cut as many as I wanted. I went to her house early the next Saturday. When I arrived, I was invited to sit down to breakfast. There was anything and everything you could imagine on the table, including a bottle of Jack Daniels in the center. It had to be one of the best breakfasts I have ever had. Before or since. After breakfast Francis's husband took me out to his shed and handed me a machete that was so heavy I needed both hands to lift it. I found a patch of small trees, maybe an inch and a half to two inches thick, just perfect for bean poles. One swing from the machete cut right through the poles. When I had gathered enough, I went back to the house; I had to ask why such a heavy machete. Francis explained that they were the first black family to move into Black Diamond in the mid 50's, and the first year they were there the town held its annual Labor Day picnic. When she and her family arrived, they were met at the park entrance by the Mayor and Chief of Police and told they were not welcome. She said her husband was so angry that when he got home he went out to his shed and made the machete, then cut down trees for the next two days.

After I got a few paychecks, Carol and I were able to buy a house in Federal Way for $20,000.00. It was an FHA foreclosure, and we had the right to buy it before it went on the market because of the settlement agreement from Lea Hills that Alva Long had arranged. Carol's mother Kay helped us with the down payment, and we moved in.

The next year and a half provided me with great work experience. Despite what detractors and Republicans might tell you, Johnson's War on Poverty was a great success. I personally know individuals and families who were able to get education, specialized training and jobs that lifted them out of poverty. Had it not been for the Vietnam war and crooks like Nixon and Reagan, I know we could have wiped out poverty in America long before we got saddled with Bush, Jr. Now I don't know if we will ever have the chance to end poverty as we know it now.

I really enjoyed being the Director of the Multi-Service Center. It gave me a chance to put into practice what I had learned in the Army and in college. I had a great group of people to work with. There was Paul from Family and Youth Services, Gail the planner and fundraiser, Claudia my secretary, the head of the transportation program, Francis Kirk with the seniors program, and several others. There was Kim Wha Plasky who had graduated from the University of Seoul with a degree in economics and a Master's degree from University of Peking in International Trade. She was Director of the Asian American Council, responsible for helping Asians relocate in the Northwest, including refugees from Vietnam. Her husband Freddie Plasky had been a German fighter pilot during WWII. He insisted he never shot down an American plane. He said he came to America after the war with $20.00 in his pocket and settled in Federal Way to open a music store. He was hired by the Board of Directors to be a fundraiser. Freddie was also friends with a lady entertainer named Bonnie Guitar, and she came to put on a fundraising concert for us that turned out to be a complete disaster. I told Ms. Guitar that it was one I owed her. I hope someday to get to repay her.

During those years, I also met Fred Lane who was the Director of the American Friends Society Native American Program. He and I have been friends ever since. He told me his mother was a Lummi and his father a Muckleshoot, so he was a Lummi-Shoot. Fred was a great guy who worked hard all of his life on behalf of Native American issues. With everyone I worked with at the Center, I can honestly say they needed no supervision because they were all dedicated to their jobs and did them very well.

One day a lady with two kids came in to see Paul with Family Services. After she left, Paul came to me and told me that an organization called FISH (Friends In Service to Him) had come to her house with a bag of groceries and a bible. They made her get down on her knees and thank Jesus for the food. It turned out this lady was Jewish. Her husband had left her, and she couldn't get on welfare until she got rid of a fairly new car he had left in her yard. The car didn't have an engine and try as she did, she couldn't sell it. To the State Welfare Department it was an asset that made her ineligible for assistance. While Paul worked on that problem, I got a statement from the lady on how she had been treated. I took the statement to United Way who was funding FISH at the time and explained how our client had been treated by FISH. After reading her statement, United Way agreed to cancel their funding for FISH and fund us instead.

In the fall of 1975, my life took another turn. The Department of Education, US Department of Health, Education and Welfare was opening a Regional Office for Civil Rights in Seattle. They were recruiting for positions in Elementary and Secondary Education and in Higher Education. My friend Bob Franco told me about it. I thought it would be a good career move, especially after talking with Carol, my friends Jerry Banchero, Vine Deloria Jr., and some others. All encouraged me to apply for it. So I did. I had two interviews. The first was with the Higher Education Branch and included about eight or ten people. They all fired questions at me for about an hour. A few days later I got a letter from them saying they had selected someone else for the position. Then I got a call from Sally Willinger, who asked me to come in for an interview with her. She was Chief of the Elementary and Secondary Branch. I met with her and she offered me a position at the GS-11 level. I turned her down, because that it paid less than I was making as Director of the Multi-Service Center. She had my qualification reexamined by the Civil Service Commission, and I actually scored higher for a GS-12 then I did for a GS-11. She offered me a position at GS-12, and I accepted.

About a month after I reported to work for Sally a request for a Federal Executive came in from the State of Oregon for someone to help them with relations between the State and Klamath Indians. I applied and had an interview with Bob Logan in Governor McCall's office. He offered me an eight-week position with the State, to write a report making recommendations to the Governor's Office on relations between the State and Klamath Indians. I thought this right up my alley and what I had been trained to do. Sally was not happy, and she had no problem letting me know how she felt. Still, I felt it was something I needed to do. She finally relented and let me take the assignment.

I went to Salem and rented an apartment. I would stay down there during the week and go home on the weekends. During my initial interview with Bob Logan, there was another individual present. He was a retired Army Colonel, and I got the distinct feeling he didn't like the project. Two weeks after I started my assignment, Bob Logan left to take another position up in Seattle. This Colonel became my new boss. I had been given an office, telephone, State car and secretarial support. After Bob left, my office was taken away and I was to work out of a supply room in the basement of an adjacent building. No more State car, but I still had secretarial support. I was also given a shadow; a young man was assigned to watch over everything I did. As difficult as it was, I was able to ditch him most of the time. I did have access to a car from the Federal Motor Pool where I would check one out for my trips to Klamath Falls. I never told my shadow when I was going, I just went.

I made several trips to Klamath Falls where I met Ms. Marie Norris, the founder of the Organization of the Forgotten American. She was an older lady in a wheelchair and a member of the Klamath Tribe. The Klamath, along with the Menominee in Wisconsin and several small tribes along the Oregon Coast, had all been terminated in the early 60's. Another thing they all had in common was that they were among the richest timber tribes in the country. Ms. Norris and her organization were providing social and legal assistance to tribal members who wanted to recuperate funds stolen from them by state banks that were appointed trustees over Klamath land. The banks were selling timber off as fast as they could, and no money was coming back to the tribe. Ms. Norris was a great help to me in preparing my final report. And best of all, she got federal recognition returned to the tribe in the late 70's. She was truly a great lady and tribal leader. I've often thought it would be a great idea to name a road, a school or a public building after her.

A strange incident happened to me on one of my trips to Klamath. I was traveling through the mountains when it started to snow. Ted George from the Seattle office of the Administration for Native Americans was with me. I looked in my rearview mirror and saw a big black truck approaching quickly from behind. I pulled over to the shoulder of the road, and eight or ten of these trucks—all black with no markings, some semi's, some pulling trailers, others with loads covered in black tarps—blasted past us going really, really fast. The trip to Klamath was easy after that since the trucks blew most of the snow off the road.

I finished my report with 11 recommendations for the State of Oregon. Needless to say, my new boss didn't like most of them and tried to make me modify my report. I wouldn't change anything. There was one item that even he found offensive; Klamath County had a road named "Dead Indian Road." He said if nothing else happened with my report, he assured me they would get the name changed. About two years ago I read in the newspaper that the name of the road had been changed to "Dead Indian Memorial Road." As for the rest of the report, I have never heard a thing since turning it in.

I often refer to my time in Salem as the time at the end of the "yellow brick road." It was truly a strange place. The people I worked with on the job were very polite, friendly, courteous and warm. On the job they would ask about my family, my job, my hobbies and other interests. However, they would never invite me to lunch or out for a drink after work. If I ran into one of them at a restaurant or store, they would act like they had never seen me before.

I returned from my assignment in Governor McCall's office in February 1976. While I was in Oregon, Sally had made State assignments for each of us new investigators. I was assigned the lead for the State of Oregon, and on my desk was a complaint filed by a Hispanic organization in McMinnville, Oregon, concerning alleged discrimination against Hispanic students in the Dayton School District. Dayton is located in farming country, just west of Salem. Mostly fruits and berries. I started by writing a letter of complaint notification to the District along with a data request. In the letter I explained the nature of the complaint, specifically the allegations that Hispanic students received disproportionately more discipline, and also that there was no bi-lingual program, no Hispanic teachers, counselors or administrators. After Sally cleared the letter, it went to Marlena, our Regional Director; once she cleared the letter, it went on to General Council for final clearance before being mailed to the District. The District responded with the data request and after review, it was determined that there needed to be an onsite visit.

I notified the Superintendent, Mr. Francis Dummer, that we would schedule two days in the District to interview school officials, students, parents and community groups. My supervisor Sally, another investigator Ricardo Cruz and I went to Dayton to conduct the review. First, we met in Mr. Dummer's office and explained our jurisdiction over the complaint, how we would conduct our interviews, how any determination regarding the allegation would be made and all the options open to our office concerning any findings from our research. I don't think the Superintendent understood a word we said. When we finished, he asked if Sally and Ricardo could be excused and if he could have a private conversation with me. After Sally and Ricardo left the room, he wanted to know what he had to do to get our investigation called off. For example, would it do any good if he were to contact his Congressmen? I told him that was his right and he should do whatever he thought best. He said he was sure that I must know how difficult it is to teach Hispanic kids, especially since most spoke very little English and some no English at all. I explained to him that Sally was my supervisor and if he wanted to have this kind of conversation, he needed to be talking to her. He replied he didn't think that would do any good.

Sally and Ricardo came back in, and we made arrangements to start our interviews. Our first interview was with the high school principal, Mr. Ellis. Again we explained to Mr. Ellis the same things we had discussed with Mr. Dummer. Mr. Ellis listened and when we finished, he offered to help us with our investigation in any way he could. He would set aside time for his students and staff to meet with us at our convenience. He also had some questions about liabilities to him and the District that we answered for him. Sally, Ricardo and I split up and went to individual interviews. I had just finished interviewing my second teacher in an empty classroom when the football coach entered the room. He was a very big man, over six feet tall with a military-style haircut. He was very angry and had me back into a corner. His face was red, and his knuckles were white. He was yelling at me, asking me what gave us the right to come into his District and tell him what to do with his Mexicans! Just at that moment Sally, Ricardo and Mr. Ellis came into the classroom. I have no doubt they saved me from a broken nose, or worse.

In the afternoon Mr. Ellis held a meeting for us with three Hispanic girls. All three were honor students or class leaders. The girls' counselor was also present. She was an ex-nun and spoke fluent Spanish from her years working in Mexico. The counselor asked the girls to tell us how things really were at Dayton High School. None of the girls would answer; they just looked down at the table. Sally spoke up and explained to the girls why we were there and what we wanted to know. One of the girls said she really liked the girls' counselor, but they all felt it would be better if they had a Hispanic counselor who understood their culture and could relate to them. They also said they didn't think the Hispanic boys were treated fairly. Mr. Ellis seemed a little shocked at their response to our questions, and he told us afterwards that he had no idea they felt that way. We held several interviews during the rest of the day, and that evening we met with some Hispanic parents and students. They told us that Hispanic boys never got through to graduation and only a few girls did. They told us that if a Hispanic boy got caught smoking on school grounds, he would be suspended. If a white boy got caught smoking on school grounds, a letter would be sent home to his parents. They also told us that most of the suspensions came during the fall harvest and spring planting time, so the boys would go to work in the fields while on suspension. The parents and students all expressed a desire to have Hispanic teachers and counselors in the high school and bilingual education for those having problems learning English.

We went back to the District in the morning and reviewed the high school discipline records in Mr. Ellis's office; they supported the parents' allegations of disproportionate discipline against Hispanic students. We then returned home after an exit interview with Mr. Dummer. When we got back to the office, we had a congressional inquiry from the Congressman representing the Dayton School District area. I was assigned the task of answering it. Sally, Ricardo and I each wrote up our findings. Ricardo had graduated from the University of Washington Law School and had just passed the Bar. He was transferred up to General Council's Office, and Jim Miles from that office was assigned as attorney for the case. After several group meetings I wrote the final letter of findings to the District and sent a copy to the Congressman. We found that the District was in violation of Title VI of the Civil Rights Act of 1964, with regards to unequal discipline toward Hispanic students and the lack of a bilingual program as required by federal regulations. The District was also in violation of Title VII of the Civil Rights Act of 1964 for not seeking or hiring qualified Hispanic teachers, administrators or counselors. The letter was cleared by my supervisor Sally, our Regional Director, and General Council's Office; then it was mailed to the District.

It wasn't long before we received another Congressional inquiry concerning our letter of findings and requesting that members of our office meet in Dayton with the Dayton School Board and the community. Jim Miles and I were selected to represent our office. The meeting was held at 7:00 p.m. in the auditorium so students and parents could attend. The entire School Board was on the stage behind a long table. Behind us on the right were white students and parents; on the left were Hispanic students and parents. The place was standing room only. Jim and I were at a little table right up front between the School Board and the community. After we were introduced by Mr. Dummer, the questions started flowing. Who were we? What was our jurisdiction? What laws were we enforcing? What were our qualifications for conducting this kind of investigation? Things like that. Jim answered all the legal questions about jurisdiction and Title VI and VII laws. I answered the rest of the questions, including what was required next. One Board Member asked how we could require the District to teach all their classes in Spanish as required by bilingual education. I explained that we were not requiring the District to teach all their classes in Spanish. Bilingual education meant that each student be assessed for language skills upon entering the District, then placed in one of six categories. Category A: speaks only another language and no English. Category B: speaks mostly another language and some English. Category C: speaks English and another language equally. Category D: speaks mostly English and some of another language. Category E: speaks only English. The bilingual requirements applied to only Category A and B. Those students were to receive some instruction in their native language, only until they were assessed to be in Category C. No bilingual education would be required after that. That seemed to calm down the School Board. The meeting lasted for several hours, including questions from the audience. When Jim and I got back to the office, we were informed that an attorney from our Headquarters Office had been assigned as the lead on this case and would be supervising all future negotiations with the District.

A little while later, we received a Title VI and Title VII complaint against the Klamath County School District from the Organization of the Forgotten American. The complaint alleged discrimination against Native American students in the Klamath County School District, especially at Chiloquin High School. Allegations included disproportionate discipline against Klamath Indians, no Native American teachers or counselors, and no Klamath tribal involvement in the Klamath County School District. I went through the same procedures in notifying the District of the complaint as I had in Dayton. Sally had hired a new investigator named Norm Nault, and he was assigned as my assistant for this complaint. The data showed no Native American teachers or counselors in the District.

After reviewing the data provided by the District, we made arrangements to visit the District. Just before leaving for Klamath Falls, I received a call from an Assistant Superintendent. He said they had taken a new survey of teachers and found they had six Native American teachers on staff. I asked him for examples of how they claimed Native American status. He said two traced their ancestry to the Mayflower and four had Cherokee grandmothers. I explained to him that the federal government accepted only three methods of proving Native heritage: membership on a tribal roll, a Native American community supporting a person's claim, or a birth certificate, baptismal or other official document. The penalty for giving false information to a federal official was a $10,000 fine and a year in jail.

When Norm and I arrived, we had our first meeting with the Superintendent, Dr. Conroy. The first thing he told us was that his assistant, the same one who had called, had had a heart attack and was in the hospital. I was devastated and in shock for a while. It wasn't until I heard that he was going to be okay that I felt any better. I never again told anybody anything about the penalties for giving false information to a federal official.

After our initial meeting with Dr. Conroy, Norm and I went to Chiloquin High School to review discipline records. We were taken to a small conference room and told that all the discipline records were in two filing cabinets. I noticed there was a mark on the tile floor, indicating there had been another filing cabinet there at one time. We spent the rest of the day going through discipline records and finding nothing unusual. When we returned the next day to finish our review, we were taken to a different conference room and there was the other filing cabinet. Inside were the records for Klamath students, and they proved that Klamath students did receive disproportionate discipline and documented a nearly 100 percent dropout rate for Native students.

Before leaving for Seattle, we held an exit interview with Dr. Conroy and told him what we had found and that the District would be receiving a letter of findings. Dr. Conroy indicated that would not be necessary. He was willing to enter into a voluntary compliance plan right then and there. We contacted the Organization of the Forgotten American, and they agreed to negotiate with the District. Norm and I went home with a plan calling for a complete review of the District's discipline procedures, initiation of an Indian Studies Program, and a recruiting program for Native teachers and counselors that included Klamath tribal participation. Since there was no letter of findings, there was no need for our Headquarters to get involved.

I recently visited the Klamath tribe and spoke with Brenda Frank, Director of Education and Employment for the tribe. She informed me that Klamath students were graduating and that the dropout rate was the same for all students. There was still room for improvement in discipline procedures, but things had greatly improved. Two Klamath members were then serving on the School Board, and Ms. Frank herself was a member of the State of Oregon Board of Education. And the District had hired Native teachers; in fact one was just in the process of retiring, having been the first Native teacher hired as a result of our compliance plan.

Shortly after my work at Chiloquin High School, I was selected for an Intergovernmental Personnel Act assignment to the Port Gamble Kallam Tribe to help them establish a Tribal Government Personnel Department. It was a year-long assignment, so I never found out what the final outcome of our efforts in the Dayton School District were since I left the Office for Civil Rights right after I completed my assignment with the Kallam tribe. I recently contacted the Dayton School District's current Superintendent, Janelle Beers, to try to get an idea if anything came from our time in Dayton. She has been very helpful and provided me with some really great news. She gave me the latest report concerning Title VI and VII activities. The Dayton School District has Hispanic teachers and administrators, two Hispanic School Board members, bilingual programs and a very low dropout rate for all students, including Hispanics. It's been a long time since we were there, maybe too long to know for sure if we made any difference or not. However, I would like to think we did. If we did have any influence in Dayton, then Ronald Reagan's assertion that the nine worst words in the English language—"I'm from the government and I'm here to help"—is just propaganda and an excuse to destroy our government. I like to believe that our efforts made a positive difference in people's lives.

CHAPTER SIX: 1981 to 1999

1981 marked the beginning of what some call the "Reagan Revolution," but what I call the "Reagan Coup." It was the successful takeover of our government by corporate interests, including how votes are cast and counted. This era explains a lot about how we've ended up with eight years of George Bush, a war, broken government, loss of jobs, declining wages and lack of allies around the world. Reagan made Clarence Thomas Assistant Secretary for the Office for Civil Rights in the Department of Education. Once Thomas was our boss, all civil rights compliance and investigation efforts immediately came to a halt. Our office in Seattle hired our own attorneys instead of using the Department's General Counsel, which in turn meant we had no independent review of our work, which as it turned out didn't matter because we were not going to do any work. Instead we were subjected to endless hours of "training" on how not to do an investigation or compliance review. We were given specific instructions on what questions we could not ask. In other words, if you don't want to know the answer, don't ask the question.

Clarence Thomas now sits on the U.S. Supreme Court and renders decisions that affect all of us. In his recent biography he is quoted as saying that his law degree from Harvard isn't worth 15 cents because he didn't get into law school on his own merits; instead he got there through Affirmative Action. If Mr. Thomas really believes that, then perhaps he should resign from the Court and let a woman take his place, a woman who got into a law school through Affirmative Action and doesn't care what anyone thinks about that. What I would recommend for Mr. Thomas is that if he wants to feel better about himself, maybe he should consider attending one of the Barber Colleges located all over the South where no Affirmative Action is required. Then he could settle down in a small Georgia town and do some good for the local inhabitants. I could recommend the same for Shelby Steele, Ward Connerly, Alan Keyes and some others who have been drinking Reagan Kool-Aid.

In colleges and universities all over the country, women now make up over 50 percent of enrollment in graduate schools, and you sure don't hear any of them saying, "My degree isn't worth 15 cents because I got here through Affirmative Action." They, like many men from various minority groups, worked hard and did what was required of them to earn their degrees. Colleges and universities receiving federal funds are still required under Title VI and Title IX to apply Affirmative Action to their admissions programs, and women have been the biggest beneficiaries. They owe no apology to anyone for getting into a graduate school through Affirmative Action. If there were no limitations on the number of students admitted to graduate schools, then there would be no need for Affirmative Action. Since there are limited spaces, schools have to make sure everyone has equal access. That's the purpose of Affirmative Action. It's ironic that some Ivy League schools are now using Affirmative Action to bring white males back into the classroom because they are underrepresented in graduate programs. Mr. Thomas climbed the Affirmative Action ladder and then pulled it up behind him. Now he is in a position to render decisions affecting millions of Americans and their access to higher education, jobs and promotions in the workplace. I'm afraid, no decision he is part of will be any good for women and minorities. Go figure!

Another factor that needs to be considered in examining Affirmative Action for women is the advent of Planned Parenthood and the birth control pill. With the advent of "the pill," for the first time in the history of the world, women had real choices about if and when to have children. Given this enhanced "choice," doors opened that had been closed to women before. This includes my daughters who have benefited from this level of choice. You can rest assured that in the event *Roe v. Wade* is overturned, the far right's next target will be the birth control pill.

In 1982, another intergovernmental position was advertised, this time with the Port Gamble Clallam Tribe. They needed someone to set up a personnel department, so I applied. Without a doubt this position was one of the best years of my government service. The Clallam Tribe is up on the Olympic Peninsula, and the people were so gracious and great to work for that I found myself not wanting to leave when my year was up. As it turned out, the tribe had contracted with a non-profit group to write their employee manual. The non-profit was doing a great job, so there was little or no need for me to interfere. I did make a few minor suggestions concerning Indian Preference, but that was about it.

When tribal governments were set up at the turn of the 20th century, the U.S. Government, through the Departments of the Army, Interior and Bureau of Indian Affairs, made sure that these governments would never become stable by calling elections for Tribal Chairman and Councils once a year. They hoped to keep these councils off balance by constantly holding elections and pitting groups against each other on a regular basis. The people of Port Gamble understood this and had made it their practice to elect the same Chairman and Councilman over and over again. Port Gamble's Chairman was Ron Charles, and many of the Councilmen and women served for several years at a time.

When I got to Port Gamble, one of the first complaints I heard was over the disparity in pay for various employees. The tribal government received operational grants from various federal agencies, such as Housing and Urban Development, the Bureau of Indian Affairs, Indian Health, Department of Justice, Department of Education and so on. When these grants were awarded, usually on an annual basis, wages and salaries were set in the grant in a mostly arbitrary way. For example, the Department of Justice set the wages for Tribal Policemen at less than half what a Kitsap County Sheriff would earn. I contacted the U.S. Office of Personnel Management, formerly the Civil Service Commission, and asked them to do a wage and hour study of all the grants awarded to the tribe. When the study was completed, it showed that tribal employees were paid 20 to 30 percent less than their counterparts in the county. Every tribal employee except one got an instant pay raise. One person was making a little more than her counterpart in the county, so the Council froze her pay until it became even with her counterpart.

One day I was called into Ron Charles's office and asked to sit in on a meeting with the Indian Health Service. They wanted to discuss a new grant for treatment of alcoholism among native peoples. They were proposing to give the tribe two Alcoholism Counselors. Ron pointed out that they had only one alcoholic, and he was already in treatment. He went on to say that what the tribe really needed were two Geriatrics Assistants to help with the tribe's aging population. The guy from Indian Health said, "No problem, just fill out the application for the Alcoholism Counselors and then hire whomever you want." I was out of my chair in a New York minute. I said, "You can't do that. That would be misappropriation of government funds and could lead to serious problems with the Justice Department." Ron asked if I would help write the grant, and I said under those circumstances I could not. After the Indian Health guy left, I continued to caution against applying for a grant under these conditions. Ron said he didn't have any problem doing what was requested by Indian Health because after all I was his witness as to what Indian Health wanted the tribe to do. I said I would be happy to be his witness, but I would not participate in any grant writing that I thought could lead to legal problems for the tribe. And I didn't.

When my year was up with the tribe, I didn't want to go back to Civil Rights, so I arranged a temporary assignment with the Office of Personnel Management to do a study of tribal governments in Western Washington. This turned out to be pretty much a waste of time. Eventually I had to return to Civil Rights, and I did. It was not good, so I did a stupid thing: I resigned from the government and went into business with my brother Harry. He had just gotten a franchise for some after-market car products and wanted me to learn the business. My brother was a big Reagan supporter and didn't think anyone should have to pay taxes. Since I was the only one in the business who owned any property, it became clear that if I didn't leave, the IRS would be after me. So I left and took a six-month temporary position with the U.S. Commission on Civil Rights.

There were four of us in the office, Susan the Regional Director, Alex my co-worker, a secretary and myself. We did accomplish one thing during the six months I was there; we held a hearing concerning Tacoma City Lights' policy of promotions based 100 percent on seniority, which was a union agreement. This meant that an African American, woman or other minority employee would have to wait about 60 years to be eligible for a promotion. We were able to get the Union and City Light to agree to a rule of three criteria for promotion, rather than the one rule, seniority. Employees would then be able to get promoted on the bases of performance, test scores and recommendations from superiors.

When my six months were up, I landed a job as Regional Civil Rights Officer with the U.S. Department of Commerce, Economic Development Administration (EDA). John Woodward was the Acting Regional Director and the one who hired me. Dr. Frank McChesney was a Division

Director in EDA and a friend of some of my friends from OCR days and he put in a good word for me, which I think got me the job. As usual I wasn't there very long before I did anther stupid thing. When I had my first interview, I wore a suit and tie. After I started work, I would just wear a sport shirt and coat. John came up to me one day and asked why I didn't wear a tie everyday like everyone else. I said, "You see, John, I was hung in a previous life, and I don't like anything tight around my neck." Everyone who heard me thought that was pretty funny, except John. I did go on to say that anytime I had to leave the office to meet with a mayor, business person or community members that I would wear a tie. That seemed to be acceptable. After that there were several people who started showing up for work without a tie.

Because I was given a reporting date of January 2, 1985, that meant I would no longer be 100 percent civil service; instead I would be in a cross-over category and partially under Social Security. That turned out to cost me $800.00 a month off my retirement. Reaganomics at work. As bad as it was for me, it's been much worse for new government employees who no longer have civil service retirement and instead have to rely on 401k's. When the stock market fails again like it did in 1929, and it will, some of these people are going to lose their retirement. They will have Ronald Reagan to thank for that.

With the exception of a few individuals, EDA was a great place to work. It was the last of Johnson's War on Poverty program and very high on the Reagan hit list for getting rid of government programs. He even mentioned EDA as a program that must go during his first State of the Union Address. He was never able to get rid of EDA, simply because there was too much support for it in Congress and the Senate. EDA would provide grants and loans for public works projects in distressed areas in order to promote business opportunities and jobs. One of the first projects done by the Seattle Regional Office was to assist the City of Ashland, Oregon in recovering from a downturn in the timber industry in the late 60's. EDA provided several million dollars for the city infrastructure to build a performing arts center. Today Ashland attracts thousands of visitors every year to their Shakespeare festival and other arts programs. Since that time EDA has helped local communities avoid or recover from economic collapse by providing public works funding, technical assistance grants and business loans. In every state in the union, thousands if not millions of jobs have been created through EDA-funded projects. EDA ranks right up with the GI Bill, Tennessee Valley Project and Rural Electrification as great American economic stimulus programs. That's not something Reaganites want to hear, but it is the truth: Americans taking care of Americans in times of economic hardship.

Among my duties as Regional Civil Rights Officer were receiving and investigating civil rights violation complaints filed in connection with any of our federally funded projects. One such complaint was filed by the African-American Collaboration in Monterey County, California against California State University, Monterey Bay in March of 1995. The complaint involved the conversion of the old Fort Ord property into a new CSUMB campus. EDA regulations required efforts be taken to provide construction contracts to local, minority and women contractors. The organization's complaint was that no local contractors were even given a chance to bid on projects at the university. My supervisor and Chief Civil Rights Officer for EDA, David Laskey, and I went to Fort Ord and met with local contractors and CSUMB President, Peter Smith, along with the person in charge of awarding contracts. We reached an agreement that the university would develop an Affirmative Action Plan for contractors and make every effort to provide contracts to local contractors. Both David and I thought the problem had been solved. But in early 1996, I received another complaint, this time from Monterey Bay Contractors Association, claiming they were still not receiving any work from the university. I went back to the university and met with everyone involved. It seemed the primary roadblock for minority and women contractors was their inability to get start-up and bonding money in order to qualify for contracts. Meanwhile, the university had hired a young attorney named Ron Cisneros as their Affirmative Action Officer. He had graduated from Harvard Law School and had been working at the university for several months. Laskey and I decided that this time we would try to mediate a formal agreement between the local contractors and the university. Through this process we were able to establish a revolving loan fund in Monterey County that would loan start-up and bonding funds to successful bidders in the local community.

In March 1996, I received word that Ron Cisneros had committed suicide. I was shocked by the news. Ron and I had been working closely on the Affirmative Action Plan, and I had received no indication that anything was wrong in his life. In August 1996 on a trip to the university, I was told by several community members that there were unanswered questions surrounding Ron's death, and they provided me with some specifics. When I returned to Seattle, I met with our Regional Director Len Smith and our General Counsel. I told them what I had learned, and our attorney instructed me to report all of it to the FBI. To not do so, given that a crime may have been committed, I could have been charged with a crime myself for not reporting it. On August 25, 1996, I filed a complete report with the FBI and was interviewed by one of their staff. I have never heard another word about Ron's death from anyone. However, I have been in the area twice since I retired and have been stonewalled whenever I mention the mediated contract agreement between the university and local contractors, or Ron Cisneros. No one will talk to me, and I have no idea why.

There was one character at EDA worth a special word or two. He had been an engineer when Reagan came into office and moved over to EDA for the expressed purpose of helping to close it down. He had everyone afraid of him. I was told to be careful of what I said around him, so of course I was all the time. Like when I asked him how he could accept a paycheck from a program he despised. His reply was that he was being paid to destroy EDA and promote Reagan's agenda. We got into a discussion one day over coffee. He was a born-again Christian. I told him that when I was growing up in scouts and in the military, I was taught that if necessary it was my duty to give up my life to protect our nation's freedom of religion principles. I said somehow I didn't think he would do the same for me. He said, "Since you're going to hell anyway, why should I die for you?" He, like Reagan, had never served a day in uniform and didn't have a clue about what being an American means. There were others in our office that were what I would call "gatekeepers." They were mostly anti-Native American and public non-profit people. One engineer who came to work for EDA said she was against Affirmative Action because too many of her white male friends couldn't get into school because of it. Here she was, a beneficiary of Affirmative Action and wanting to pull the ladder up behind her just like Clarence Thomas. She was also anti-Indian fishing rights because some of her family members were fishermen. She was a gatekeeper; when she didn't like a particular project, she would employ delay tactics, lose a file here, misfile something there, keep asking for the same information over and over again, until the grantee just got tired and gave up.

Under Reagan we were not allowed to fill in after retirements and other vacancies. Instead, we were required to double up on duties. When Bush Senior became President, we were allowed to fill some vacancies as long as they were acceptable Republicans. One such individual was appointed as Economic Development Representative for Southern California. He was a real gem. When I first met him, he said he took the job to insure that government standards and ethics were upheld. Later I learned he went to law school on government time and earned a law degree while accepting a government paycheck.

Then there was the Inspector General appointed by Bush Senior. Under his watchful eye we were subjected to very close scrutiny. Our Assistant Secretary was a political appointee named Orson Swindell who now sits on the Federal Trade Commission Board and is dutifully carrying out the "Reagan Coup." He was always putting out memos saying that federal employees accepting gratuities would not be tolerated in his agency. We were not even allowed to accept a free cup of coffee, this in spite of federal regulations allowing business lunches of up to $25.00 in value as long as they were business related.

As one of my projects I worked in Boise, Idaho with a non-profit that had developed a light industrial park with an EDA grant. The lady I worked with was Ann Beebe; she was Director of the non-profit. We had negotiated an employment plan to hire disabled workers and minorities among the several businesses there. For example, the hotel chain in the park had hired developmentally disabled people to clean rooms. The manager of the hotel was so pleased with their work that he had recommended to other hotels in the chain to hire disabled employees. After our tour of the hotel, we went to a neighborhood Mexican restaurant, and although I told Ann I had to pay for my lunch, she insisted she would pay for it. When I got back to the office, I mentioned to John Woodward what had happened at the restaurant. He instructed me to put it down in writing and give him a copy. I did and in my report I wrote, "The only way I could have made Ann take my six dollars for the lunch was to knock her down and stuff the money down her bra, and I just was not going to do that." A few days later I got a call from Ann wanting to know what was going on. She had an IG inspector from Denver come to her office and demand to know how much money I had extorted from her agency to get the project funded. I asked her what she did; she said she threw the bastard out and told him never to come back. I never heard anymore after that. So much for standards and ethics in government. This is a great example of Reagan/Bush political ethics.

Then came Clinton. We went back to doubling up on jobs because we were not allowed to fill in vacancies. At this time I was given the added responsibility of Economic Representative for Southern California. I would spend the next year dividing my time between the Regional Office in Seattle and our office in Los Angeles. It was way too much for one person to do. By this time John Woodward had been transferred to Denver, and Len Smith had been promoted to Regional Director. When I first came to EDA, there were about 350 EDA employees; about one third of all the managers were African American. Over the years I witnessed that number fall steadily; as people retired, their positions were left vacant. I reached 30 years of service in 1999 and decided it was time to retire. EDA was no longer any fun, and everyone was being asked to do way, way too much to be effective in their primary duties. I think that was the intent. No, I know that was the intent.

Today, Len Smith is the last African-American manager left in the agency, and the Bush Administration is working hard to get him fired so they can replace him with a Reagan/Bush Republican. Here is a man with 30 years of exemplary performance who is suddenly receiving negative evaluations. Not only that, but the Bush Administration is violating the Hatch Act, which says there can be no political test for the appointment to a civil servant position and that civil servants are subject to very strict laws limiting their political activities. EDA, like I suspect most every other federal agency, is now required to refer any vacancies to headquarters to be filled by political appointees with individuals loyal to President Bush. If this is indeed a widespread policy among other federal agencies, then it would amount to the wholesale sell-out of the Hatch Act. Hatch Act violations provide for very stiff penalties and should be investigated by Congress and the FBI.

If and when the Democrats take back the White House, the House and Senate, and if they decide that EDA is a good agency operating in the public interest and opt to keep it, I would recommend they appoint Len Smith as Assistant Secretary for EDA because he is quite frankly the only one left with the institutional memory to return EDA to its great and historic role of serving distressed areas and communities.

In 1999, after 30 years of public service and continuing Reagan-Bush politics, I decided to pack it in and retire. Financially I should have waited until I was 65 to retire, but given how the government was going I could not see how staying was going to make any difference to anyone. So I retired and started a new life minus $800.00 a month from my retirement check, thanks to Ronald Reagan and his war on entitlements, which are hard-earned retirement benefits and disabled veterans' compensation. Of course, dividends from invested capital and not earned by hard work are quite another thing.

WHAT HAVE WE GOT TO BE SO SMUG ABOUT?

Among our presidents we've had:
Slave owners
Burglars
War criminals
Ethnic cleansers
Liars
Adulterers
Thieves
And at least one idiot

CHAPTER SEVEN: 1999 to Now

I'm retired now and loving every minute of it. Everything, that is, except eight years of Bush Junior. Who would have ever thought that a spoiled frat boy like him could not only end up in the White House, but single-handedly destroy our government institutions, take us into an illegal preemptive war against a country whose major asset is oil, and have the nerve to tell the American people a bunch of lies and get away with it? This is a guy who deserted his National Guard Unit, couldn't pass the SAT to get into the University of Texas and went to Yale and Harvard as a legacy. By the way, if I had graduated from either of those two schools knowing he had too, I would be wondering if my degree were worth 15 cents. George Bush has blood on his hands, and so do Cheney, Rove, Wolfowitz and others in his administration. Like many of my friends I think they are nothing more than common criminals, and I really don't understand why they are not in jail. I suppose I *know* why they're not, I just don't *understand* why they're not. There's another one of those "whys."

I've been to Mexico twice and Nicaragua once. I could live very, very well in either place on my retirement income. Only thing is, I would have to leave my family and friends behind, and I have come to the conclusion that I couldn't do that. While I would like to travel more, my home is here, and here it is going to stay. My daughters, son, grandsons, granddaughters, walks around Seward Park, fishing, bicycling, lunch and poker games with my friends, holiday dinners with my family, and sunsets are all too important to me to give up. So, here I am and here I stay, and I know why.

Since retiring I've started helping my daughter Kristin with her silkscreen business. After graduating from Western Washington State University with a degree in design, she started helping my cousin Nannette with her screen business in Issaquah. They later moved into my garage while I was living in Issaquah. When I moved, Kristin had already established her own business. We moved her business to my old stomping grounds in "Garlic Gulch," otherwise known as Rainier Valley, and we have been there ever since. Sometimes the business has been a struggle, but we keep trying to find that magic formula for success.

YOUNG ONCE

I was young once
Never thought I'd grow old
Then one day I woke up
And I was old
Damn

TRIBUTES TO FAMILY

I can't imagine what my life would have been like if I not had the family and friends I have had. They have gently guided me, shoved me on occasion and pushed me when necessary, successfully most of the time, but not always. Somewhere along the line I figured out that the Cleaver family didn't really exist and that life is unpredictable for most of us. I have also concluded that life may be unpredictable, but family and friends have the power to help us through the most trying of times and at the same time bring us great joy and happiness.

As I wrote in the Introduction, this book is all about my attempt to say "THANK YOU," to my parents, sisters and brothers, spouses, children, nieces and nephews, cousins and many wonderful friends. Since my parents were the first influence in my life, I will start with them.

Sigurd Dagmar Swensen and Bertha Longden Swensen
1916

My mother Bertha was born on November 28, 1895 in Duluth, Minnesota where she also grew up and went to school, including a secretarial college. She died at age 95 on Valentine's Day. I am sure it was her intent to pick a day we would never forget. There weren't many opportunities for women when my mother was growing up: teacher, nurse or secretary, and that was about it. Oh, well, there were two other professions, one of which was housewife, and my mother became one in 1916. She had three sisters, Marion who was older and Martha and Dorothy who were younger. My mother and Marion were the only two who had children of their own. Marion had a boy Henry and a girl Muriel. We are still close with Henry's children and grandchildren. My grandmother Katherine came to America from Ireland and married Harry Longden who came here from England. I came across some pictures of my grandfather's sisters; they were dressed in typical Jewish dress of the time, according to my neighbors who were Jewish. My grandfather had joined the Masons, so we suspect he converted sometime before marrying my grandmother.

My mother was a very outgoing person who loved people and especially entertaining, family dinners, friends over for cards, socializing with the neighbors, canning fruits and vegetables, anything that had to do with being around others. She started out working at the Bon Marche in the Shipping Department and later was promoted to running the Layaway Department. That was during a time before credit cards; people would pay a little down and a set amount every month to the Layaway Department until the item was paid for and then take it home. My mother was also a great cook, except for her spaghetti. She insisted on putting stewed tomatoes in the sauce, and I never understood why. Another one of those mysteries.

Later in life after my father died, my mother sold their house to my nephew Scott David Winslow, my sister Jane's youngest son, and his wife Gretchen. Our mother then lived with my sister Toodie part of the year in California and with my family in Bellevue the other part of the year. She had been raised a Catholic but had left the church long before I came along. Since my sister Toodie is Catholic, our mother started attending church again, and I think it gave her a lot of comfort. I couldn't have asked for a better or more caring mother than the one I had. She gave me far more than I could have ever returned.

My father Sigurd was born in Deerwood, Minnesota on October 12, 1892, the first child of Hans and Joakima Svendsen to be born in America. My grandmother's heritage was Sami, a reindeer-herding people of the Norwegian Arctic. When my father was very young, his family changed the spelling of their last name to "Swensen." Like many immigrant families did upon coming to America, they Anglo-sized their name. My father, also like many others from immigrant families at the time, went to school only through the third grade, but that never stopped him from working and achieving business success throughout his life. Even during the Great Depression, my family never stood in a bread line. My father sold the *Book of Knowledge* to professionals like doctors, attorneys, accountants and bankers. My mother and sisters traveled with him all over the country, selling books, living in hotels and driving long hours from city to city.

He often told a story about when he was in Kansas City calling on a banker to sell him accounting books. During their conversation, the banker made a rude remark about book salesmen. My father told the banker that he had just toured Kansas State Prison and was told there were over 30 bankers doing time and not a single book salesman.

My father was the second of ten children. First there was Hilda, who was married and moved away from the family, never to be seen again. Some think she was murdered by her husband, but nothing conclusive ever came of it. Then came Lydia, Alvin, Esther, Harvey, Agnes, George, Julia and Louis. Aside from my Uncle Alvin and Aunt Agnes and her daughter Millie, we never saw much of my dad's side of the family, mostly because they all live in the east.

After WWII, my father started Swensen-Case Company and bought and sold printing equipment. During weekends and summer vacations my dad would hire some of my friends, like Dale, Richard, his brother Al and some others, to help him move heavy stuff like paper cutters and presses. One Friday, my dad hired Dale and I to go to Tacoma to pick up a paper cutter he had purchased from a print shop. When we got there, the owner told my dad that he wanted to sell the whole business. My dad asked how much he wanted, and the guy said $20,000 cash. My dad asked if he could use the telephone, and he called his bank in Seattle. At the time it was Pacific National. He made arrangements to have a bank draft in the amount of

$20,000 sent to the Tacoma branch of Pacific National. $20,000 then would be like $200,000 today. I learned later that my father had gotten a loan, but he didn't go into his branch to sign papers for the loan until the following Monday. His word was all it took to close the deal. Try that today. When the check arrived, the former owner went around to turn everything off. He took off his apron, handed over the keys to the door, cleaned out the cash drawer, and left. All the while we were cleaning out the place, people were coming in looking for their printing orders, which of course we didn't have.

While attending high school and working at the health food store and meat market, I had another job at Jack's Fish Market, picking up fresh fish for him everyday. One day Jack asked me if my father was Sigurd Swensen. When I said yes, he told me about the time he moved into our neighborhood in 1952. There was a restrictive covenant in place that said no one could sell or rent to Jews or Negros, and no one could own chickens. Jack was also Jewish; I remember when someone dumped garbage all over his lawn and painted Swastikas on his front door and garage door. Jack told me there was a petition going around to get him out of the neighborhood and that my dad and one or two others were the only ones who wouldn't sign the petition. Several of our neighbors had chickens, but I never heard of any petitions to get rid of them. It wasn't until the mid 70's when African Americans began to move onto our block.

My dad died in 1979 at age 87 after spending the last two years of his life in a nursing home. His memorial service was standing room only. All kinds of people we didn't know but who knew him were there with great stories about my dad. There never was I time when I needed some kind of help, money, car fix, whatever, that my father said no. I have tried to be as good a father as he was; in thinking about it I'm not sure I can be, but I try.

SISTERS AND BROTHERS

There is not much to say about my sister Dale and brother Harry. Dale had three girls: Barbara, who is a few months older than me, Linda, who married my friend Jim Garl's brother Danny, and Chris. Linda and I are still pretty close, but I don't see the others much. My brother Harry had two girls by his first marriage to Marge, Kathy and Lynn; we also don't see as much of each other as we should. Harry also has two sons, Harry Jr. and Howard. We have never met Harry Jr. and met his brother Howard only once.

My sisters, Shirley "Toodie" and Janie, I love both dearly. Janie died a few years ago, and I really miss her. She was the youngest girl and had two sons, Calvin Jr. and Scott. Cal has a PhD in History and has spent his life teaching. Scott was also an educator and administrator; he also recently passed away. Janie, her two sons and their father Cal were all politically active and very successful in their careers. We always had the best discussions about politics and current events. Janie and her second husband Marv built a summer cabin on Puget Sound with my father's help. Marv was Business Editor for the *Tacoma News Tribune* and a great brother-in-law. I learned so many things from Janie and him on our weekend visits. What a great place. There were so many memorable hours spent clam digging, oyster shucking, fishing, eating great food and drinking good wine. I bought a waterfront lot a short distance away but was never able to do anything with it other than camping with the girls and their friends on weekends.

My sister Toodie will turn 88 this year, so we are planning a birthday party and family reunion for this summer where she and husband Marvel live in Penn Valley, Northern California. That is, if we can find a cake that will hold that many candles. Toodie and her first husband Clifford had seven children. Judy, the oldest, died of breast cancer in her mid-forties. There was also her brother Dennis who now owns a movie industry research firm. Kathy, a school teacher, had two children, Shawn and Ann-Marissa, both of whom are newly minted attorneys. Brian is a musician who has played with Seals and Croft, Ike and Tina Turner, and many others. He is currently appearing at Dollyland in Tennessee. I start everyday listening to his wonderful piano recording. Marianne owns a painting business with her husband Jim and works for the State of California. Theresa is a very successful tarot card reader, and Priscilla plays in the Santa Cruz Symphony Orchestra.

My sister Toodie still remembers coming to Seattle in 1925. They all traveled by car on mostly dirt roads since there were few paved roads and no freeways. There were long distances between towns so they camped out every evening. When they were crossing the plains, she saw large herds of wild buffalo. Something no one will ever see again.

My brother Forrest is truly one of my heroes. He's five years older than me, so we were never really close growing up. By the time I was a teenager he was serving in the Navy, and when he came home, he got married. The reason he is one of my heroes is because he has overcome many challenges in his life and has always given his family and friends far more than he has ever taken. He has two daughters, Marlene and Cindy. Marlene is developmentally disabled and a constant source of problems. Forrest and his second wife Donna have been raising their granddaughter Katty, who was also born with challenges. She just completed high school, has a job and is learning to live on her own. Cindy works for a school district, and her husband Jim is a musician.

My brother retired a few years ago; his wife Donna and some coworkers held a retirement party for him at the Renton Eagles. My sister Janie had gotten Forrest a job with King County Roads Department when he got out of the Navy, and he put in over 30 years. In a packed banquet room, his supervisors, co-workers and many friends and neighbors came forward and told the most loving and interesting stories about my brother, stories that I and the rest of our family never knew about him. It was one of the proudest days of my life to see a side of my brother that none of us knew existed.

CAROL

Carol died in her sleep, February 12, 2003, on Kristin's 35th birthday. There is much I can say about Carol. She was the very best of mothers. She was a great partner. She was a great daughter and daughter-in-law. She was gracious, tolerant and helpful to anyone anytime she could be. She was also troubled. She was in a serious car accident and suffered a head injury around 1964; I think that is when her mental health problems began.

Even though she had been diagnosed schizophrenic, which is usually hereditary in nature and comes on in the early teens, Carol's parents told me she had shown no symptoms until after her car accident. Why they didn't tell me about her condition when I first met them, I will never know. Except, I think they took any sign of a family member with mental illness as something personal. Carol's aunts, uncles and cousins acted like she didn't exist. Some of them went so far as to say they didn't want her around. When the girls were 11 or 12, Carol decided she couldn't live at home anymore and moved in with her mother and then on to a friend's before going to Keystone House, a group home where she lived the last years of her life. While it took over three years for her to get in, I know Keystone was one of the best things to happen to Carol. She had good treatment, and her friends and family were around her.

After Carol died, Kristin and Cary held a memorial for her on Mercer Island. Every member of her family, including her mother, refused to attend. There were 40 or 50 people who showed up to pay their respects. Sorority sisters, childhood friends, co-workers and some of my family and friends came to say goodbye. A week or so later, a memorial was held at Keystone House. She was happy there. The staff had been mostly able to keep her on her medication, and she could come and go as she pleased. Kristin and Cary spent time with her nearly every weekend, and she would call me two or three times a week. It's difficult to explain, but I think Carol and I grew closer than ever during those calls.

At the memorial at Keystone House I experienced the most spiritual event of my life. There was a woman minister who must have known Carol well and spoke eloquently about her life. She then passed around a single flower and told everyone there that when they got the flower, they could speak about Carol or pass the flower on. There were about 40 or 50 seriously mentally ill patients in the room. Also my friend Jack, Kristin, Cary and myself. Jack had missed the memorial on Mercer Island and so insisted on coming to this memorial. When the flower came to him, he said, "In all the years I have known Carol, I have never heard her utter a single word against anyone else." It didn't take me a second to realize that he was telling the exact truth; she never did. Then it happened. A young man, a patient, got the flower and told us the story of a time when he had been thinking of committing suicide and decided to go outside for one last cigarette. When he got outside, Carol was there smoking her cigarette, and they talked for about an hour. He said after their conversation he no longer wanted to commit suicide. No one from Carol's family was there to hear how Carol had affected a seriously ill person by helping him overcome an urge to kill himself. How many of us can say that we ever impacted someone else's life in such a significant way?

It is shameful how we treat the mentally ill among us. There was a time in America when we had a plan to open halfway houses for the mentally ill across the country. But when Reagan got into office, among the first things on his agenda was to kill that idea. We now have thousands of mentally ill people wandering the streets of every city in America and local communities trying desperately to find a way to help them, which I don't believe can be done in any effective way without federal planning and support. Local communities are just not up to the task.

TO MY KIDS, WHO ARE NO LONGER KIDS

One of the lessons I learned from my teacher and friend Vine Deloria Jr. was that we all belong to a tribe of one sort or another (there's that Indian thing again). This is not the only way of looking at family and friends, but it is one that makes sense to me. My sister, brother, aunts, nieces, nephew, cousins and friends are the ones who make up my tribe today. We hunt, gather and eat together, we dance and sing, we cry together. We are all in some way dependent on each other. I find this aspect of my existence to be very reassuring. I have no idea where I would be without them, especially my children and grandchildren. I only know I wouldn't want to be there without my four children, Candie, David Jr., Kristin and Cary, and my four grandchildren, Rachael, whom I have never met, Gracie, Mitchell and Jesse.

There are some events in life that happen, and we never get over them. Such is the case with Autumn taking Candie and David away from me. I will never know if I did enough or I should have done more. The only thing I know is that I have lost Candie and my granddaughter Gracie, maybe forever. They have chosen to take a different path in life and one that I cannot follow them down. My only hope is that someday one or both of them will come to value our family enough to make some changes in their own.

After years of separation my son David and I became acquainted in 1985. He was two years old the last time I had seen him. He had just joined the Air Force when we met at Castle Air Force Base in California. We got off to a rocky start, and it took a while to get to know each other. In fact it was Kristin and Cary who wrote to and talked to David the most during his six years in the Air Force Police. He would visit them during the holidays. During his time in the Air Force he served in England, Honduras and Cyprus. When he got out in 1989, he came to live with us, and I have gained not only a great son but a great friend. I hear him talk and I think I'm listening to myself. He married his girlfriend Vicki who had helped with my court case against John L. Scott. They now have a son Mitchell and live in Tucson, Arizona, where he is a building engineer and going to school. I feel bad that I missed out on David's growing years, but there are no words to describe my joy when he came to live with us and now seeing him whenever I can. David, Kristin and Cary are very close, and nothing can make a father happier than that.

When Kristin and Cary's mother left, I had to sort out how to be a single father. I wish that I could say I was the World's Greatest Single Father, but I can't. It wouldn't be true. It's not that I was a bad single father; it's that I had a lot of help. My mother would come and spend summers with us. Kristin and Cary's grandmother Kay spent a lot of her time with the girls, and of course we had our friends. Most of all, the girls still had their mother. They kept in contact, and the girls got a great start in life because of their mother. Our house was the center of the neighborhood. When they were in high school, the girls both worked to pay for their own stuff. Kristin was a lifeguard at a local swim club, and Cary worked after school at the school district building. When Kristin was 17, she wanted to become a lifeguard at the swim club, but the manager told her she couldn't because she was too small. I told her, "You don't ever let anyone tell you what you can't do. You try, and if it doesn't work out, it's okay because you did try." She did and was a lifeguard there for the next four years.

I had to travel a lot during that time, so the girls' grandmother Kay would look in on them. Still there were some interesting events, like the time I got home and my neighbors asked me why the police and fire trucks were at my house while I was in L.A. It seems the girls thought it would be a good idea to have a party. It got out of hand when uninvited guests showed up and caused trouble. It was Cary who called the police to break up the party, and for that reason the police just broke up the party and didn't do anything to the girls except to warn them about unsupervised parties.

In 1985 after I had started work at the Economic Development Administration, I had to go back to Washington D.C. to meet my new Civil Rights Chief, David Lasky. I took Kristin and Cary with me, and we stayed with our friend Bob Franco. His daughter Marine and the girls are the best of friends. Bob took us all around D.C. and even to Thomas Jefferson's Monticello. We joined a tour group led by a lady who looked to be over 100 years old. She told the group that Jefferson had built Monticello. I said to the girls, "Now you know Jefferson didn't build Monticello, his slaves did. However, he did design it." When we were a little further on in the tour, the guide pointed out where the servants' cabin had been. I said to the girls, "Now you know these were not servants' cabins, they were the slave quarters, and one of the slaves, Sally Hemming, is rumored to have had children by Jefferson." At this point the tour guide became very agitated with me and asked us to leave the tour, which we did. For some people the truth is just not acceptable for young children.

During their junior year in high school, the girls' cousin, my great niece Dawnn, came to live with us; she and her sister Jamie are members of our tribe in good standing as well as my cousin Nannette and her children, Lynnette, Terry, Mike and Kelly with whom we spend every Thanksgiving and Christmas Eve. Nannette introduced Kristin and me to the silkscreen business.

After high school Kristin went to Bellevue Community College where she earned an AA Degree and then transferred to Western Washington State University where she earned a BA in Design. Her sister Cary went to Western right after graduating from high school and was already there when her sister arrived. They roomed together while Cary earned a teaching degree. With the help of our friend Vine Deloria Jr., Cary went on to the University of Colorado to earn a Master's Degree in Women's History. She is now Director at a Sylvan Learning Center and substitutes at local schools. Kristin has a silkscreen business and is a real estate agent. She has a three-year-old son Jesse.

Can any parent be more proud of David, Kristin and Cary than I am of them? I don't think so; other parents might be just as proud but certainly no prouder. Children are our legacy and when they do good, we feel good. You can't get better out of life than that.

TRIBUTES TO FRIENDS

Friendships and snowflakes are unique.
If you look close, they contain great beauty
stored in their individual design.
Handle friendships with care and they will stay with
you for a lifetime.
Mistreat friendships and they will melt before your eyes,
like a snowflake, never to be seen again.

I am not sure I could have made it this far in life had it not been for friends. Many times I've needed help, mostly in the area of advice, building confidence, sharing of experiences, and just plain listening to my sad tales of woe, sometimes even financial. I've had far too many friends to go into great detail about all of them right now, but some of my dearest friends include the Fenkners, Richard and Al, Dale Bond, Paul Gouge, Willie Green, Gail Wright, Gene Palm, Rob Muse, Lenore Threestars, Freddie Lane, Claudia BeBee and so many others. Below are tributes to some fabulous friends I've had over the years.

JERRY BANCHERO

One of the first people outside of my family to affect my life was Jerry Banchero whom I came to know through Boy Scouts Troop 222. Jerry's father owned Mondo Meats where my mother bought her meat through the war and into the late 50's. Knowing Jerry has enabled me to know most of his family, his mother Nellie, brothers David and Lew, and their kids. Jerry died several years ago, and since then I have missed our conversations over a glass of wine at his wine shop. Jerry was truly a unique individual; he was six foot seven, a graduate of Santa Clara University, a Lieutenant Colonel in the Army Reserve and owned a wine shop in Rainier Valley (Garlic Gulch) that hosted a wine tasting every Wednesday night. The place was always packed with the most interesting individuals, actors, astronauts, doctors, politicians. People from all walks of life, people with all kinds of different views on good wine, the Vietnam War, the economy, politics, religion, etc.

Jerry was fluent in every subject, and he had no problem letting anyone know where he stood. For me, what made Jerry unique was our ability to differ to extremes on subjects like the Vietnam War and religion. He was a devout Catholic and yet completely tolerant of my non-religious feelings; he never took it personally. Some of the best conversations I had on the subject of religion were with Jerry. He was also a patriot who took great pride in his uniform and was ready to serve his country whenever and wherever. I, on the other hand, was completely against the Vietnam War and our country's involvement there and was willing to demonstrate against it. And yet, no matter how much we differed on any subject, it never affected our friendship. It just didn't matter. Maybe that was because when I was editor of the *Fort Lewis Ranger*, Jerry was a second lieutenant in a Fourth Infantry Unit. We used to have coffee in the Headquarters Building. One day Jerry's Company Commander called him in and told him he was not to see me again. He would not tolerate fraternizing in his unit. Jerry told his Commander that we had been friends since Scouts and that the Army was not big enough to tell him he couldn't have coffee with his friend. A compromise was reached when it was decided that he and I could meet as long as we were in civilian clothes and off the base. Which we did.

There was also the time when Jerry, Dale Bond and I took my car and went to a carnival in Issaquah. We had some beer in the trunk and would make trips back to the car all day long. When evening came, we started home only to find that I had left the lights on and the battery was dead as a doornail. While we were trying to figure out what to do, the Sheriff pulled up and asked us what we were doing. We explained and he told us to get in the back of his car. While we were driving down I-90, he was on his radio with the Seattle Police. We were sure we were going to jail. When we got to the floating bridge, there was a Seattle Police car waiting with two officers in it. All three of us were near panic. We got in the police car, and the officer on the right turned and asked us where we lived. The collective sigh of relief almost blew the windows out. In any case, Jerry and I had a history, and with history can come mutual respect, tolerance for different opinions and most of all an appreciation that friendships are far more important than opinions. Although it goes without saying, I truly miss our conversations and his counsel.

LEW AND SUZY BANCHERO

I have known Lew and Suzy for many years through Lew's brother Jerry. Lew took over his dad's meat market after his dad died. His brother Jerry's wine shop was just a few doors down the street. Just like my mother bought meat at Mondo and Sons, I also bought meat from Lew, mostly for special occasions, like lamb for Easter, or prime rib and New York steaks for Thanksgiving, Christmas and New Year's. Or ribs for a summer BBQ. I would see Lew at Jerry's Wednesday Night Wine Tasting, and over the years a family friendship has grown, including with Lew and Jerry's mother Nellie as well as with Lew's three sons, Mondo, Angelo and Mario. My daughter Kristin and I have rented space from Lew for our silkscreen business, and Lew and I now have lunch together several times a week. The lunch times I spend with Lew are truly "quality time." Lew is the only person I know who can argue both sides of most any issue and still manage to win both sides.

Suzy is a school teacher, and Lew is in a perpetual state of early retirement. His sons are taking over the business, making Mondo's a third generation business and one of the oldest in Rainier Valley. Both Lew and Suzy have contributed much to their community through their church and active participation in disability causes and other community services. All three of their sons are carrying on this family tradition. Lew and his family are among a small group of people who give back to their community in a regular and sustaining way. Rainier Valley is a far better place because while others fled the Valley in the 60's and 70's, the Bancheros stayed, built their businesses and created a great place for their kids to grow up. They now live in a "house that Lew and Suzy built." It overlooks Lake Washington, so every year during SeaFair they invite friends over to see the Blue Angels Air Show. Garlic Gulch is where I grew up, and it's been an important part of my life ever since. Lew and his family have made it a better place for everyone.

JACK WYLIE

My friendship with Jack goes back to Sharples Junior High. If Jack had been born into a Native American tribe, he would have been designated Tribal

Historian or Chief Storyteller. No one I know can tell a better story with more detail than Jack. Ask him what time it is and he will ask you, "Do you want sundial time or wristwatch time?" I can honestly say that spending time with Jack is always a gift of time well spent. Everyone comes away feeling a little better after one of Jack's stories.

Jack and I used to spend early summer mornings going down to the Seward Park fish hatchery and fishing until about noon. It didn't matter if we caught anything or not, there was sure to be a good story coming out of it. After high school he graduated from Edison Technical School with a degree in auto mechanics. Later we were in the National Guard together and went on six months active duty together. Jack was there when I fell off the mountain. He was there when I needed a place to live after leaving Autumn. Currently Jack is an auto mechanic and recently retired from Boeing. He has a garage out behind his house and spends his spare time helping his family and friends who are having car trouble. I couldn't begin to tell you how many times Jack saved me from huge car repair bills. And I'm not alone; the list of people he's helped would be 10 times as long as any of his stories. Actually, getting Jack to work on your car is a real social event and a true learning experience. One time I had a boat with a four cylinder in-board motor, and I blew a head gasket. I took the boat over to Jack and asked him if he could fix it. He said, "No, but I'll show you how to fix it. You buy the parts, and I'll show you how to fix it, and it won't cost you anything." That's when I learned just how hard fixing things can be. I did get it done though, and the motor ran just great.

After high school Jack had a girlfriend named Gail. Gail introduced me to Marty, and we dated for a while. Marty found her true love, and I moved on. Gail and Jack eventually split up and went on to raise separate families. But they are together again now and have the most wonderful love story to tell about how they got back together. If you don't know it yet and you meet Jack, be sure to ask him to tell you how they got back together. For anyone who thinks things can never work out, their story will be an inspiration to you. Yes they can, and sometimes they do.

BILL MCINTYRE

I first met Billy when I worked in the Office for Civil Rights around 1978; he was an attorney in the Department of Health and Human Services. We had mutual friends, Ricardo Cruz and Jim Miles, both attorneys in the same office but working for the Department of Education. It didn't take long for Billy and I to become friends. Because we're both disabled vets, we had a common place to start. When I asked him how he got his disability, he would only say it was a jeep accident. It wasn't until 1999 that he would be able tell me or anyone else the whole story.

Billy had joined the Army in 1956, and they wanted to make an officer out of him. But he kept refusing, so finally they sent him to Army Intelligence School where he was taught cryptography. After completing school he was assigned to England Special Services Unit where his cover story was that of a football player for an Army team. In reality he was assigned to spy on East German and Russian Troops in East Germany. Billy's mother was Mexican, and he grew up speaking fluent Spanish, so the Army gave him another cover story. He would be a Spanish exchange student attending the University of Leipzig in East Germany. His job was to travel around East Germany and use a transmitter he carried in his backpack to report troop movements. In his backpack were textbooks on top, Playboy magazines in the middle, then more textbooks and his transmitter on the bottom. Whenever he was stopped and searched, the guards never got past the Playboys and always confiscated them, then let him go on his way.

Billy said his greatest fear was the German dogs trained to sniff out Americans. When he would cross the border either coming or going, he could hear the dogs barking in the distance. He was on the way to cross the border when the driver of his jeep lost control and the vehicle rolled over. Unconscious, Billy was taken to a West German hospital where he was in a coma for three months. The hospital authorities couldn't identify him as an American soldier because his ID said he was a Spanish exchange student. He had a shoulder bone punctured through his lungs and other injuries. When he came to, he was able to call his Company Commander, get released from the German hospital and sent to Fitzsimons Army Hospital in Denver, Colorado for treatment. When he was discharged from the Army, they told him he could not tell his story for 40 years. He had to keep his secret from everyone, including his family, under penalty of prison and being forced to repay his GI benefits, such as education benefits and any GI home loans.

After leaving the Army, Billy earned a law degree while working for the Department of Health, Education and Welfare. During his career as a government attorney, Billy recovered over $30 million dollars in overpayments of taxpayers' money to doctors and hospitals receiving Medicare benefits. During his federal career the injuries he suffered while on active duty had gotten worse, and he was later granted full disability. However, because of Reagan's means testing for military disabilities, he now receives compensation at 50 percent of a 60 percent disability. What Reagan meant when he said "to get government off your backs" was to stop the government from recovering misappropriated taxpayer money and to cut benefits to our nation's veterans as much as possible. Reagan never served a day in uniform. Billy retired from federal service after his work continued to grow because his agency was under a hiring freeze and working conditions were impossible. Billy's wife Marge retired from a position as County Parole Officer after her caseload grew from 60 to over 300.

Billy is a true hero who served his country both in uniform and out. Like many other veterans he deserves better than what all these flag-waving conservatives are willing to give.

THE KHALIFES

I really got lucky when we moved to Bellevue from Federal Way. Freddi and Polly Khalife lived next door, having just moved to America from England. Our dog Brown-b was the first to meet them. Freddi would have olives, cheese and fruit on Saturday mornings, and Brown-b would go through their garage to their kitchen door and mooch. It wasn't long before I was going through their garage to the kitchen door and mooching, only I was mooching on intellect and friendship. Freddi was a French citizen and Polly a British citizen. However, both were raised in Alexandria, Egypt. Freddi worked for a very large international insurance company with a specialty in ships and international trade. He was one of those rare individuals who can see the forest from the trees. No matter how we differed on any subject, he never took my position personally nor did I his. We could even discuss issues between the Israelis and Palestinians without getting angry, something I think few people are capable of today. The subject seems to be either one way or another with no in between. It seems now that if you dare to say anything against Israel, you're immediately labeled an anti-Semite. If you say anything critical of the Palestinians, you're anti-Arab. We can no longer have a rational dialogue on the subject, especially when the leaders of our country refuse to talk about it. There is so much I learned from Freddi and Polly. Everyone should be so lucky to have such neighbors.

Just before Freddi was to be vested in his retirement plan, his company fired him to get out of paying his retirement benefits. He was very upset, and his son Frank was just coming home from New York. I suggested they file a complaint with the U.S. Equal Employment Commission and get them to conduct an investigation into Freddi's situation. I also told them not to let the commission make any kind of findings in the case because the commission almost always found in favor of the employer. By withdrawing the complaint after the investigation had been completed and before a finding was rendered by the commission, they could hire an attorney specializing in employment issues, which they did. The attorney took that investigation report and won a settlement with the insurance company. Shortly after that Freddi and Polly moved to Hawaii where Freddi was killed while jogging by a reckless driver.

Their son Frank and I have become close friends, and Frank's sisters Marilyn and Sandra and Frank's wife Ronda taught my daughters Kristin and Cary things girls need to know about make-up and such. Frank is now a CPA and does our taxes. He's also one of our poker-playing buddies. We see Polly whenever she comes to Seattle or we go to Hawaii.

FRANK McCHESNEY

Frank knew me before I knew him. I was looking for a new job, and my friends Ricardo and Billy were friends with Frank. Frank was Planning Director at the Economic Development Administration when he called me and suggested I apply for the agency's Civil Rights Officer position. I did, and I got the job. That was in 1985; a friendship was born. Frank had been the Economic Development Representative for the State of Washington and would later serve as EDR for the Pacific. Frank was a WWII Navy veteran. He was a graduate of Penn State and the University of Pittsburgh and held a PhD in Political Science from the University of Washington. Frank knew government and how it was supposed to work. Because of his knowledge of planning principles and implementation methods, he was able to advise Washington State Native Americans and Pacific Island Natives on creating and funding very successful economic development programs that lead to business opportunities and jobs. Because of Frank, people's lives got better. Frank recently died. However, he left me with very fond memories of many, many lunches together. He left me with a greater understanding of what it means to be a "public servant." Of all the people in EDA I think he personified the very best of what an agency designed to provide economic assistance to distressed communities should be doing. Frank also had a great sense of humor. I can say with absolute certainty that after a lunch with Frank the world and my place in it looked a whole lot better. We all will miss him.

ALDA

I can honestly say I never knew what a woman could teach me or how she would accomplish it until I met Alda. I'm not trying to be demeaning towards women; of course, I have learned a lot from them. It's just that what Alda had to teach me I didn't see coming, and it would change the way I look at women in my life before and after her. Alda was in my life for only a short time, but the lasting effects still have me a little bewildered.

I had moved into a condo on Mercer Island, and even though Alda lived right below me, it would be several years before we got to know each other. We had seen each other going in and out of the building but had never talked. It was on a bus trip home from work that I happened to sit next to her, and we began a conversation. We started dating shortly after. It only lasted a little over a year, but what a year. I was on a perpetual high. I couldn't wait to get home from work and go for a walk or dinner with her. She had graduated from Stanford and the University of Minnesota. After Stanford she worked for the CIA and was stationed in Saigon during the late 1960's. After that she got married and raised a family in the midwest. When her family was raised and she got divorced, she moved back to Mercer Island where she had grown up. Her family was very conservative and didn't like me much; some were even downright rude to me. I didn't care because I enjoyed her company so much her family didn't matter. And maybe I was a little rude to them also.

Alda moved out of our building and bought a condo on Capital Hill. I would go see her after work, and we would spend most of the week together. It was there at her condo that she told me she was having an old boyfriend from her CIA days come and stay with her. It was over. At this point I went "crazy," not literally insane, just a little "crazy." I sent her flowers, which I had never done before. I wrote poetry; I even published three copies of a book for her. I started riding a bike, attending the Seattle Symphony and trying some other things she liked to do that I never had. My friends and family were very understanding and attributed my behavior to a simple mid-life crisis. Maybe they were right, I really don't know. Just as I was getting over things, Alda moved into a condo a block away from me. I couldn't go out without running into her. It was really hard. So I decided to sell my condo and move. That in turn set off a chain of events that would last for the next seven years and make some Washington State real estate law in the process. Alda eventually moved back east, and I would guess she is doing quite well for herself. As for me, I'm still writing poetry, some good, some not so good, riding my bike whenever I can, and going to the symphony regularly. Who would have ever thought that I had poetry, bike riding and the symphony in me, or that I would enjoy them all so much? They are truly gifts that I have Alda to thank for. She is one of those people who made my life better, and I will always be grateful for that.

GEORGE PURDY

Sometimes you have to stand up to make a bully sit down.

Friendship can come from any direction: childhood, school, scouts, the military. And sometimes they grow out of a professional relationship, such as attorney and client, which was the case with George and me. George is a partner in Simburg, Ketter, Sheppard and Purdy, a firm that specializes in real estate law. In 1995, I needed a real estate attorney in the worst way. A mutual friend recommended George, and out of our legal struggle came a very significant consumer protection decision by the Washington State Supreme Court as well as a very good friendship.

It all started when I made the decision to sell my condo, move off of Mercer Island, away from Alda, and buy a house in Issaquah. My son David's girlfriend Vicki had just started selling real estate, and I would be her first customer. She found a house on a corner lot in Issaquah that I wanted the instant I walked in the front door. All on one level with a sunken living room, three bedrooms and three baths, one of which was perfect to turn into a sauna. Vicki wrote up my offer, and it was accepted. She noticed that on the disclosure form there was a question concerning flooding on the property. The sellers had marked "yes," but then scratched it off and marked "no" at the direction of the seller, agent and John L. Scott Real Estate. Vicki sent a fax to the seller's agents and got back a reply that it only meant there was occasional "puddling" in the driveway when a car was being washed. I moved in and started doing some remodeling. I was at work when I got a call from my contractor telling me that my garage, car and driveway were all underwater. When I got home, I found that most of the stuff I had stored in the garage while waiting for the remodeling to get done had been ruined, and water had soaked most of the inside of my car. Fortunately, I had moved all of my books in the house the night before. However, I had been working on a book about single fathers, and all of my transcripts were destroyed along with family pictures, birth certificates and other important papers. Most of it was irreplaceable. I called Vicki, and she called the seller's agent who came right over and saw the damage that had been done. She said she would contact her broker and get right back to me. Needless to say, days went by and I never heard a word. The seller's broker was John L. Scott Real Estate, and they informed Vicki that they weren't going to do anything about the flooding. They would not pay any damages or repair any problems with the property. At that point my only recourse was to hire an attorney.

George came out and saw the damage done by the flooding; in the process we discovered that the water had come from my next door neighbor's yard. There was a surface water drain pipe buried in her yard that had overflowed. We learned later that the same pipe had a history of overflowing and that apparently no one owned it. We also learned that the John

L. Scott agent had sold the house before and knew about the flooding problem. George contacted JLS and tried to negotiate a settlement, but their attorney Douglas Tingvall refused any discussion on the matter. He left us no choice but to go to court. George filled suit in early 1996, and we began our seven-year journey.

The legal process requires an attempt at mediation. Somehow I had learned that Tingvall was an amateur opera singer, so when we held our first and only mediation meeting, I told him about my singing career. I told him that in junior high school I had signed up for boys choir, thinking it would be an easy "A." The second day the teacher called me down from the risers, walked me to the door and told me to try woodshop. He was sure I would like that better. Everyone in the room laughed except Tingvall. I knew right then, despite what everyone said about him being the best real estate attorney in town, that he was an amateur attorney as well.

We went to trial in District Court in 1996. We decided on a six-member jury out of 18 candidates. During the jury selection period I asked if we could know who the jury candidates' heroes were. Everyone laughed at my request, but the judge said it would be okay. Some said their fathers, some said Ronald Reagan or Jesus, but others said Gandhi, Martin Luther King, Caesar Chavez and Robert Kennedy. When the jury was selected, there were no Reagan, father or Jesus worshippers on it. The trial lasted a week, and Tingvall never cross-examined anyone or put up a single witness on behalf of his agent. I've often wondered who Tingvall's client really was. Was it the agent or John L. Scott Real Estate itself? The jury came back with a unanimous decision: John L. Scott and their agent had committed "fraudulent concealment and other consumer protection act violations." The jury also decided on a monetary award; I thought they would just write a check and that would be that. No way. Tingvall was going to take this all the way to the Supreme Court.

At this point I was really pissed. I didn't have any more money to go further with the case. George wanted to go on and offered to take the case the rest of the way, but I had another plan in mind. It was clear to me that since JLS had forced many others besides me into prolonged legal battles, it was their intent to intimidate anyone who would challenge them in court. I decided on a public relations campaign to inform sellers and buyers about the dangers inherent in doing business with JLS. I printed up flyers and started handing them out every Sunday in front of JLS open houses. I also set up a website with the whole sad story (www.realestatealert.net). The result was a front-page story in the *Seattle Post Intelligencer*, radio show interviews and a significant drop in sales for JLS. My efforts had another effect I hadn't counted on: All the publicity educated the courts on JLS's business practices. When we finally got to the Washington State Supreme Court, we won another unanimous decision. The Court ruled nine to zero in my favor. The website is still up and informing the public about how JLS does business. As far as I am aware, JLS has not taken anyone to court since they lost this case and instead have opted to settle claims at the mediation stage. JLS and Tingvall kept me in court for seven long years. They have never apologized, and I suspect given the chance they would go back to their old ways.

George and I have become friends, and he has since helped me with good legal advice and good conversations on many subjects. And in case anyone is wondering, here are my heroes:

Sir Thomas Moore because he wouldn't give up his religion.
George Washington because he wouldn't be King.
Crazy Horse because he wouldn't give up his land.
Caesar Chavez because he wouldn't give up his union.
Rosa Parks because she wouldn't give up her seat.

VINE DELORIA JR.

If we are really lucky, every now and then someone comes into our lives and leaves a lasting mark. Vine Deloria Jr. was such a person for me. I had read his book Custer Died for Your Sins before coming to Western and meeting him at the College for Ethnic Studies. I still wasn't sure about Indians, even though I had spent a year working with kids from the Muckleshoot Reservation and helping Green River Community College to develop a recruiting program targeted at Native Americans. Green River after all was my first experience working with Native Americans.

To get into the College of Ethnic Studies you had to be interviewed and have recommendations from a community group. The Muckleshoots had recommended letting me in, and Vine interviewed me. This is where my education really began. Everything I thought I knew about African Americans, Asians, Hispanics and especially Indians was almost completely false and based on fear, racial stereotypes and just plain old ignorance. This turned out to be a journey of enlightenment that changed my life forever. When I graduated from the College of Ethnic Studies and began working, the world looked different to me than before I started.

In Vine's books, in his classroom and in the hours working as his teaching assistant, I came to understand that America does not always live up to the promises in the Constitution and Bill of Rights or the promises of the 1960's and 1970's for equal opportunity. For example, while working as a Civil Rights Investigator, I had a large school district's Assistant Superintendent tell me, "If you make us hire niggers, we're going to hire the most unqualified, ill-prepared niggers we can find, and when they fail and they will, I'll see to that, we'll just blame it all on you feds for forcing us to hire them." I was shocked that he would use such language while speaking directly to a Civil Rights Investigator. That is something no Assistant Superintendent would ever say to a minority or a woman, but because I'm white he somehow thought I would understand how he really felt about Affirmative Action and the hiring of teachers. Unfortunately, I come across white Americans nearly everyday who would agree with that Assistant Superintendent and even say, "right on."

Vine knew the importance of the academic study of the ethnic experience in America for everyone, not just for minorities and women. He knew that until ethnic studies was universal and part of every curriculum, there would always be those like the Assistant Superintendent. Racism is still alive and well in America, it's just that people are more careful about the face they show in public. Reagan and both Bush administrations have gotten away with the total emasculation of civil rights protections for all minorities in American institutions.

After my graduation Vine hired me to do research at the UW Law Library, various newspaper files, and from other sources around the Northwest. Whenever he came to town for a meeting or speech, he would stay with me, and we would continue my education. In many of his books and at all speeches I attended he encouraged young people to continue the struggle for their inherited rights. They should know their tribal history, how native people solved problems, provided for the general welfare and how they treated each other and their neighbors. They should know that lying was the most serious offense a tribal member could commit and that it almost always led to banishment.

Vine would tell his audience that lying was a serious matter because people's lives depended on the truth. I believe this to be true today just as much as Native Americans did before the white man came along. In the pre-colonial history of this land, anyone caught in a lie would lose any credibility they would otherwise enjoy. Because they didn't have paper to compose agreements, a person's word was his bond. While that did persist for a while in America, like when my dad bought out that printing company, I don't think you will ever see that kind of thing happen again. As for lies in general, native people were not prepared for the European and American versions of the truth. That's where the expression "white man speaks with forked tongue" comes from. After a while native people came to understand that lies were part of the game they were being forced to play. Like with Port Gamble Clallam Tribe and the Indian Health Service. Can you imagine living in a world in which lies were unacceptable and could lead to banishment? What would advertisers, oil and drug companies, the State Department, CIA and especially politicians do then? Vine knew and I know we can never expect our society to embrace such a radical idea as always telling the truth. However, each of us has the capacity to always tell the truth or in the absence of that never knowingly tell a lie. Such a simple and easy principle to live by. I know there are people who could never live without lies in their everyday lives. But for those who can live without them, how much more enjoyable life can be.

Vine would point out to his audiences that second in importance to not telling lies was developing the ability to recognize lies. Anyone who has ever watched a John Wayne western movie or a television drama about Indian people has been exposed to lies about the native experience. We need to recognize when we are being lied to and do something about it. If nothing else, let others know you've been lied to. A good example would be to point out a lie that John McCain is telling veterans. He claims to support veterans in their struggle for health care and other benefits they have been promised; at the same time, in his tenure as a U.S. Senator, he has never voted for a single bill benefiting veterans. Or when you see a lie being told by a drug company commercial, be sure and let your doctor know that you know it's a lie.

A year or so before working with the Port Gamble Clallam Tribe I was at a convention of Native American scientists and engineers at a hotel in Seattle, and Vine was the keynote speaker. There were several hundred recently graduated Native Americans and many large corporations there recruiting these young men and women. Vine told the young people that they would be taking positions where at one point or another they might be asked to do something contrary to their culture. In order for them to know the right thing to do, they should turn to the nearest native community and ask for advice from tribal elders. While I was at Port Gamble, a young Native-American man approached me and asked if I remembered what Vine had told the audience at that convention, and I said yes. This young man was a Seneca from New York and an engineer at the Bangor Torpedo Station nearby. He told me to tell Vine that he had he gone to the Port Gamble elders during a time of need, and they had solved a dilemma for him. He never told me what the dilemma was, but he did go on to say that he was volunteering as a math tutor for native students in the area, which was another thing Vine had encouraged these young professionals to do.

Those are but a few of the lessons to come out of knowing Vine. Besides a great sense of humor, Vine had the ability to listen to what others had to say and bring meaning out of racial hatred, bigotry, intolerance, misinformation and plain stupidity. I witnessed him time after time turn someone around and get him or her to consider another point of view. I don't believe anyone who has read one of his books or heard him speak would ever think of Native Americans the same as they did before.

Vine would also confound people who thought they knew him. When my daughter Cary graduated with a teaching degree, Vine invited her to apply for a teaching assistant position he had open at the University of Colorado. His program would allow her to earn a Master's in Women's History. All she had to do was apply to the university's history department. She did and after the fourth rejection, I called Vine and asked him what Cary should do. He said he would take care of it, and in a few days Cary got an acceptance letter. The department was not happy with Vine's choice of teaching assistants. They had selected two native students for Vine, and Vine had selected two non-native teaching assistants. In this case the head of the department was clearly playing the role of gatekeeper, something native people have been subjected to by the American government and others for over 200 years. She was deciding what was best for Vine and my daughter. When Cary arrived, the head of the department told her that because she had not taken a foreign language in college, she would be required to take two years of college-level foreign language or she couldn't be in the program. I'm sure they thought this requirement would send Cary packing. But they didn't know Cary. She signed up for two years of Spanish. This meant that she would be there for four years, including writing her Master's thesis, which she did. She wrote her thesis on "The Role of Native Women in the Washington State Bolt Fishing Decision." As far as I am aware, it is the only work done in this area of the Bolt Decision.

I know Vine's life's work, his writing, teaching and friendships have had a lasting effect on the well-being of native people, their rights and their historical impact on American society. Without question, his life's work and our personal friendship have had an ever-lasting effect on my life.

ROBERT FRANCO

Robert and I met when we both decided to go to Green River Community College in Auburn and buy houses in Lea Hills. When we met, his name was Robert Johnson and he was just out of the Navy. He changed his name back to his birth father's name when we were going to Western Washington University in Bellingham. Robert served in Vietnam during the war and as a Navy Corpsmen; among his duties was preparing killed-in-action soldiers and sailors for shipment home. My friend Jack's stepfather had similar duty on the beaches of Normandy during WWII. He had to pick up bodies and body parts, stack them in a pile and burn them. It's too bad George Bush never had to perform such duties. Maybe if he did, we wouldn't be in Iraq right now.

Robert and I had a lot of adventures together. We worked for changes in how veterans were treated at Green River Community College and on the Homeowners Association at Lea Hills. When we were getting ready to go to Western, our families didn't want to go to Bellingham, so Robert and I rented a house together close to the university and came home on the weekends. I can still remember the great conversations we had about politics, religion, public service, war and peace on our trips back and forth from Bellingham. After graduating with a degree in political science, Robert went to work for the Civil Service Commission and climbed the ladder to Senior Executive. He's retired now but still travels all over the world as a consultant, giving classes to other senior executives on diversity in government. Since he lives in Virginia, we don't see each other much anymore, but we keep in contact by email and telephone.

RICARDO CRUZ

Ricardo and I became friends when I met him at the Office for Civil Rights at the Department of Health, Education and Welfare. He had just graduated from the University of Washington Law School and was waiting to take the Bar. It was a time when I really needed a friend. Here I was, a "white boy" doing civil rights work. Some in the office didn't like that idea and made it clear to me that I could never understand what women and minorities have gone through or even begin to comprehend discrimination. Sally told me she hired me only because she couldn't find a qualified Indian (there's that Indian thing again) and because of a recommendation from Vine Deloria Jr. I don't know what a "qualified Indian" is, I just know there are a lot of people looking for them. Ricardo was the guy I went to whenever someone put a wake across my bow. I always got good advice from Ricardo and still go to him today seeking his counsel.

THINGS I THINK ABOUT

After being around for as long as I have, I have some thoughts on the subjects of guns, government, education, healthcare and God that I'd like my family and friends to hear. My thoughts come from my formal education, work experience and day-to-day living, but mostly from my associations with everyone around me: those I love and admire, and those few self-righteous, self-centered know-it-alls who can never seem to make it out from their own shadow. You know, the ones who are always right and never have the capacity to listen to another point of view or be influenced by it.

GUNS

I grew up around guns. My father kept them in an unlocked closet where I could and did bring them out from time to time, just to look at them. Ammunition was in the drawer next to the closet. Fortunately, the thought of getting bullets out never occurred to me, but it could have. I guess I was just lucky, unlike some 3,000 children and teens killed each year by guns. Like my friend in junior high school. Estimates run as high as 100,000 people suffering from gunshot wounds each year, with half of those being fatal. That's about 275 people per day being shot and 135 dying from the wound. Day in and day out. The Vietnam War lasted about 10 years and killed 59,000 young American soldiers; that's about 16 soldiers a day. We honor those brave Americans with the Vietnam Memorial in Washington D.C. Where is the wall to honor those who die each day because the NRA tells us "guns don't kill people, people kill people"? Had guns not been so available, hundreds of thousands of people would be alive today. Parents would have seen their children grow up, fathers would be around to help their families, and scores of families and friends would have been spared countless hours of grief and suffering, not to mention the millions of dollars that taxpayers would have saved in healthcare costs, social security benefits and funerals.

Our family had a recent experience with a gun. When a gun was brought into our family, my daughters and I decided to get rid of it. The gun was legally registered, and I learned that if I turned the gun over to the King County Sheriff, it would only be returned to the owner, this despite the fact that the owner claimed to be bi-polar, wouldn't work and had mood swings. The gun was also kept in a place easily accessible to his two-year-old son. I wrapped the gun up in cardboard and tossed it into Lake Washington. I was later accused of stealing the gun. The Sheriff's Department called and asked if I had the gun, and I said "no." The Sheriff asked what I did with it, so I told him I tossed the gun into Lake Washington. There was a long pause, and he finally said, "You did what?" I told him again, and he told me he would have the Sheriff's Marine Division contact me. When they called, I told them where I had tossed the gun and agreed to meet them at the spot. I wasn't sure if I would be going to jail or not, but I met them there, and they found it on the bottom of the lake. During that meeting the deputies told me there were only three reasons to deny a gun permit to anyone: the person was a convicted felon, legally declared mentally ill, or have had a no-contact order from the courts filled against them. None of these applied to the gun owner in this case. So I concluded I had done the right thing. Off the record the deputy agreed. In any case the gun is now locked in the Sheriff's property room with a tag requiring a court order for it to be released. During this ordeal one of the deputies asked me what I did for a living, and I told him my daughter Kristin and I had a silk screen business. A few days later we got a $2,500.00 order for t-shirts from the Marine Division.

I have found that all the reason and rational discussion in the world will never convince a gun owner to give up his gun. It's just not going to happen. Does anyone think it would help if every newspaper in America ran a running death toll by guns in America on their front pages every day? It may not help, but it would get some attention for the subject outside of the NRA. What I would like to see is a federal law requiring "liability insurance" on every gun sold in America. Local communities could decide on the amount of insurance required; obviously there are differences in gun ownership between Fargo, North Dakota and New York City. We require liability insurance on cars, motorcycles and boats. Mortgage holders require liability insurance on homes, so why not on guns? Insurance companies would make sure that a mentally ill person or a felon wouldn't be able to get insurance and therefore no gun. If an accident happened resulting in injury or death, at least the victims would be eligible for some kind of compensation. That in turn would save taxpayer money in the form of social security benefits and Medicare. Of course, the "gun show" loophole would also have to be shut down. Anyone caught selling a gun without insurance attached would have to pay a very stiff penalty. The same would hold true for anyone caught carrying a gun without liability insurance.

I know I am saying all this at the risk of having my front window shot out, but sooner or later America is going to have to do something about our insane gun lobbies and inadequate gun laws. I am sure that if rational people sat down to discuss this issue, a reasonable law protecting an individual's right to have a gun and protecting innocent people from death and injury could be developed. It's just never going to happen if the NRA is part of the discussion. Maybe liability insurance isn't the whole answer, but I sure think it would help.

GOVERNMENT

A HORSE FOR THE COMMANDER AND CHIEF

Let's get him a horse
Our commander and chief
Let's get him armor
This commander and chief
Let's get him a spear
This commander and chief
Let him go into battle first
Let him show the way
This commander and chief
Let him spill his blood first
This commander and chief
Who deserted his own army
Let his loved ones mourn first
This commander and chief
Let all those who want war go first
Let them mix their blood with oil
Let them go first
With their commander and chief
With his horse
His armor
And his spear

"WE THE PEOPLE" doesn't always mean "WE THE PEOPLE." In far too many cases, it means "WE, SOME OF THE PEOPLE." Some get way more privileges than others. Some people serve their country, some don't. Some people go to jail, some don't. Some get healthcare, some don't. Some get education, some don't, and so on. The extent of privilege that a person enjoys mostly depends on how much money he or she has. The more money, the more privilege. In the last half century we have seen the ranks of "WE THE PEOPLE THAT DON'T" grow and grow. This has happened before in America. It happened in the late 1800's and in the 1930's, and it's happening again. The wealth of our nation is flowing upwards to a very few, instead of down to the people. When I was a kid growing up in

Rainier Valley, we never had homeless or mentally ill people walking our streets or sleeping in our doorways. Most families in our neighborhood never even locked their doors. I saw our cities and neighborhoods deteriorate after the Vietnam War. I can't help but believe there is a direct connection, mostly because I see it happening again with Iraq vets.

The current downward trend started with Ronald Reagan and his mugging of America. When he said, "We need to get government off our backs," he didn't mean "our" as in you and I. He meant the backs of the polluters, banks, the oil, drug, and chemical industries, the Wal-Marts of the world. The two Texas Bush's, who have or are now serving in the White House, have extended Reagan's mugging to outright rape, to assault and battery. Believe it or not, right now these administrations are guilty of attempted first-degree murder against the federal government. They have set out to destroy as much of the government as possible before they leave office.

I have seen this destruction with my own eyes. I have felt the pain of honest dedicated civil servants who not only struggle to *keep* their jobs but even just to *do* their jobs. Grover Norquist, a senior neo-con advisor to Reagan and both Bush's, came right out and told us what they intended to do. He said, "Our goal is to cut the government in half in 25 years, then down to a size such that we can drown it in the bathtub." Reagan, the Bush's, Cheney, Norquist and all those supporting them have been desperately working to build a bridge to the 18th century and the era of the "robber barons." They are very near completing that bridge, and you and I are going to be the ones forced to cross it. It's because of them that we don't have enough air traffic controllers, meat, bridge and port inspectors, teachers or policemen. It's because of them that oil, chemical, pharmaceutical, financial and other industries all across America go unchecked for anything resembling an interest in the public safety or welfare. Their only interest is and always has been their friends in oil, at Halliburton and Kellogg, Brown and Root. They have plundered our national treasury unchecked and unaccounted for, and outright stolen billions of dollars from you and me the taxpayers in no-bid contracts and a general environment of corruption as business as usual.

They have violated so many national and international laws. They have completely disregarded the Hatch Act as it applies to the hiring of federal civil servants. Passed in 1939, the act was intended to protect civil servants from being forced to participate in partisan politics and carried with it very stiff penalties including prison. The Bush Administration, across the board in every federal agency, has thrown this law out the window and will now hire only individuals who pass a loyalty test to George W. Bush and no one else.

Of all the crimes committed by this administration, by far the worst is the torture of POW's, or prisoners of war. Bush and his gang have completely destroyed any moral or ethical standing America ever had in the world. If there is any one single crime they have committed that they should go to jail for, it is this one.

When I worked for Lucker Meat Market as a teenager, my boss was a guy named Hans. In 1944 Hans was a cook aboard a German submarine, which was captured off the east coast of America. He spent about two years in an American prisoner of war camp at Fort Bliss, Texas. Hans became a trustee and was allowed to leave the camp every day to go to work in an El Paso meat plant. I remember asking him, since he could have escaped into Mexico anytime wanted to, why didn't he? I will never forget his reply. He said, "I had a job, and my earnings were put into trust for when the war was over. I had three meals a day, a job and a warm place to sleep. Why would I have wanted to escape?" After the war Hans had enough money to send for his family back in Germany, and he became an American citizen. That's the America I put a uniform on for. Hans made me proud to be an American. If I were to go overseas on vacation now, I would learn to speak Canadian and try not to let anyone know where I really come from.

EDUCATION

THE TREE OF KNOWLEDGE

If you burn the tree of knowledge
To keep warm in the winter
There will be no blossoms
In the spring and summer
And no fruit in the fall

What is it that Western Europeans and people from many other countries know about education that we don't? Do they know that their national treasure and the wealth of their nation reside in their citizens? Do they know that an educated population brings prosperity in many forms, including global business, cultural preservation, lower crime and world leadership? I have no doubt that they do. Why can't we see that? I conducted an experiment recently: I asked more than 20 people, friends, acquaintances, just people I would meet here and there. I asked, "What would you do to improve education in America?" Not one mentioned anything about No Child Left Behind. They all said pay teachers more or lower class size, and some said both.

It seems that most people know how to solve our educational difficulties, except those professional educators, politicians and school boards who refuse to deal with both of those issues. I also have several male friends who claim they would have chosen education as a career, except they didn't think they would be able to support a family on a teacher's salary.

An interesting fact: The current starting salary for a non-supervisory teacher in the Seattle Public School Teacher is $34,426.00 and requires a four-year college education, plus state certification and continuing education to be completed every year. Some teachers have as many as five classes per day with 30 plus students each to teach. That's 150 kids plus per day that some teachers have to interact with. I don't care how dedicated a teacher is, that's an impossible task for anyone. Why is it that when we have put the future of our kids in their hands, we have decided not to give teachers a living or family wage?

Seattle Police Officers, on the other hand, have a current starting salary of $57,503.52 plus a 20-year retirement program. To qualify for this position, one needs a high school diploma and six months at a Police Academy.

If we want to know the value of an educated population, just look at the GI Bill following World War II. Our country was facing 20 million young men coming home from war, with no jobs and many with as little as an eighth grade education. Also don't forget that they knew how to use guns. Experts thought it would take two or more years for our factories to retool from making tanks to making refrigerators, and all these men were going to need housing. The GI Bill provided educational opportunities by expanding existing colleges and universities, and new colleges and universities sprang up across the country as well. Housing projects were built to house students going to school. The greatest generation was being rewarded for their service, and our country had some breathing room. The result of all this was the greatest investment any country could make. Nearly everyone's lives got better. We got doctors, teachers, lawyers, accountants, nurses, scientists, businesses, farmers and builders, all of whom paid back their GI benefits, a thousand times over in increased taxes and other revenue to the government. The GI Bill gave me $300.00 per month for 36 months to get a college education. That totaled $10,800 in education benefits from the Bill. My accountant, Frank, estimates that over my working lifetime, I paid between 20 and 35 percent more in income taxes than I would have without my education. Multiply that by the hundreds of thousands of veterans who increased their taxes paid by the amount of education received, and show me a better return on any investment dollars. Reagan and the Bush's have cut the benefits for returning veterans and made the program voluntary. Some take advantage, some don't. Housing benefits in the form of Veterans Home Loans are gone altogether.

Today, with the advent of excluding student loans from bankruptcy, we have a proliferation of private schools that are signing up young people for thousands of dollars in student loans for training anyone can get at a community college or public trade school for a tenth of the cost. For example, a friend's son just signed up for a two-year police training program in a private college for $50,000 a year in student loans. That's $100,000 plus interest over two years for a questionable education. My friend's son could have gone to a community college for an accredited education with certified teachers for about $2,700 a year, a total education cost of about $5,400 dollars. He could have saved himself about $95,000 plus interest. Bush Sr. called this kind of film flam "voodoo economics," and he was right.

In addition to more pay for teachers, smaller class size and higher education for everyone, we should consider what we are teaching our kids. Anyone coming here from another planet and reviewing our public school curriculum would conclude that we are an almost totally white society. We celebrate "Black History Month" each February, and most of that time is spent studying the life of Martin Luther King. We celebrate Thanksgiving by telling grade schoolers about how Indians (there's that Indian thing again) saved the Pilgrims, and of course we celebrate Cinco de Mayo with tacos served for lunch in high schools. We should be teaching our kids the truth. The plain truth is, there is no part of American history that has not been touched by hands of color; African Americans, Indians, Asians, Hispanics and Pacific Islanders have contributed to everything that is American. When we teach our kids about America, we should be teaching them everything about America. They need to know about the contributions of all minority groups to history, the arts, science, math, business, government and the military as well as their participation in all aspects of our democracy. If we are really serious about mending wounds existing in all Americans, then I think this is where we start.

HEALTHCARE

Americans didn't have the best healthcare in the world prior to Reagan, but it wasn't so bad. Most hospitals were non-profit corporations; drug company's and the insurance industry were well regulated. Drugs were made in America and subjected to rigorous testing by the Federal Drug Administration before they could be prescribed by doctors. Most employers paid for employee health insurance and employees could contribute to premiums to get additional heath insurance for their families. The system wasn't perfect, but it worked. Then came Reagan and deregulation of the entire healthcare industry. Hospitals turned into profit making enterprises. Drugs are being made overseas, are not subject to safety standards, and have been put on the market without proper testing. The insurance industry and drug companies hit the "jackpot." Huge profits, excessive CEO compensation, forty-seven million Americans without any healthcare at all, and many times more under insured. The insurance industry alone takes out thirty to thirty-five per cent of every dollar for administration and profits, compared with three cents taken out of Medicare Insurance for administration and nothing for profits. Medicare is a Government run healthcare program that works. The insurance industry is like a dead drain on a batter that doesn't work.

Simply put, what we have now is ***not*** a healthcare provider system; it's a healthcare ***denial*** system. Because, even if you are lucky enough to have health insurance, your insurance company is going to deny any claim they can get away with in order to maintain profits and dividends for administrators and stock holders. The leading cause of bankruptcy in America is unaffordable healthcare. The Republican response to that has been to tighten up bankruptcy laws and make it harder for families to file for economic relief.

I recently went for a dental examination at a local "Garlic Gulch" dentist. There were three people working at the reception desk. I was taken into the exam room where a dental assistant set me up for the doctor. He came in and poked around in my mouth calling a number for each tooth. When he finished, the assistant took four or five x-rays. The doctor came back in and said he had *"good news and bad news."* It seemed that I needed some extractions and deep cleaning, and partials. He said he would prepare an estimate of what it was going to cost me, since I don't have dental insurance. I came back in a week and he gave me the news. The initial visit to get the estimate cost $271.00. He told me I was looking at a six month treatment program and it would cost me $12,000 dollars – maybe more. That is one big chunk out of my retirement income, and I just couldn't see how I could afford it. Another *Garlic Gulch* friend suggested I do what he did. Go to Victoria B.C. and check out the dentists up there. I went online and found one in Victoria who would see me. I made a reservation on the Victoria Clipper and arrived at his office. There were two people there: the receptionist and the doctor. I was taken into a examination room, where the doctor poked around in my mouth and took four or five x-rays. He came up with the very same *"good news, bad news."* He asked me to wait in the outer office for a few minutes. I hadn't even had time to begin reading the paper when he called me back into his office. He outlined the same treatment plan, only it would be done in three months and he guaranteed it would not cost more then $5,000 dollars – maybe less. His examination fee was $126.00. So now I am scheduled to take a two-and-a-half hour boat ride to Victoria once a month for three months to get the work done. Would I prefer to do business in *Garlic Gulch*? Absolutely. Will I pay $7,000 more to do it? Absolutely not.

Healthcare has been an issue in American politics since Theodora Roosevelt first introduced "*universal healthcare*" in the first Social Security bill in the 1930s. The Republicans got it removed from the bill. President Truman tried again in 1945 and again the Republicans beat back any attempt for a National Healthcare system. In 1965, Medicare Insurance for those over sixty-five was enacted as part of President Johnson's ***"WAR ON POVERTY"*** In 1972 the disabled became eligible for Medicare. I remember the 1965 Congressional Hearings on Healthcare for the elderly. I remember senior citizens testifying that they had to eat dog food in order to pay for their medical treatment and drugs. Most Republicans in the House and Senate at the time voted against passage of President Johnson's Medicare bill. I would guess none of their parents were eating dog food in order to pay for medical treatment or prescription drugs. Early in the Clinton Administration, Hillary Clinton tried to bring us a National Healthcare system and the Republicans handed her her head. Maybe she will have better luck next time. I certainly hope so for all our sakes. It has taken more then thirty years to include drugs in Medicare coverage and how did it get included? The drug industry wrote the bill for Medicare Part B, which is just another giant *"rip off"* and profit making source for them. It only covers certain drugs made by certain companies and even my local pharmacist can't explain it to me. He just says *"this plan covers these drugs and this plan covers those drugs."* God help you if you need drugs from two different companies and don't forget the co-pays and deductibles.

Even the Veterans Administration is reneging on their trust responsibilities to our nation's veterans. In 1985 a very high ranking Veterans Administration official told me to stay away from the VA. They were under orders to cut as many vets from their rolls as they could. A short time later I was called into a VA administrator's office and asked it I had private health insurance. I replied that I did in order to cover my family. She told me I could not us my VA medical benefits at the VA hospital any longer. I would be required to use my private insurance. Right at that time I knew exactly how Native Americans felt before the ink even dried on their treaties. (There's that Indian thing again, only this time I knew exactly what it meant.) The Reagan Administration had put an eight category system in place, which meant that the closer you were to number eight the less treatment you would receive from the VA. If you were category eight of course you got nothing. It was VA administrators and doctors who determined which category you would be in despite any previous determination for eligibility.

Needless to say I don't go anywhere near the VA. Who knows what Iraq and Afghanistan veterans are facing with their VA medical benefits. I only know it can't be good.

No discussion about healthcare in America can be complete without considering what we as Americans put in our bodies and where it comes from. I know as a kid growing up my peanut butter and jelly sandwich, banana and milk were healthy for me. Even if at the time I would have gladly traded them for almost anything. I think we had one fat kid in our class and of course his name was *"Tubby."* Today more kids are overweight then not. Drive by any school and see for yourself. Most everyone would agree that the culprit is processed and fast foods. Few if anyone has any idea of where the food in our stores comes from, much less what's in it. Because there is little or no Federal oversight in our food production systems, we have no idea of what pesticides, steroids, or other dangerous chemicals have been used on the foods we are buying. Even worse, we have no idea of the long term effects they will have on us or our kids. Neither does our current Government and that's because they don't care. Food and food products are coming to us from all over the world, with no inspections or compliance with any kind of public safety standards. Republicans keep telling us that this is a good system because it brings the consumer cheaper food products. Well, I've got news for them. I just paid $2.19 for one tomato at my local grocery store.

I am one of those overweight Americans who used to drop by my local McDonalds for a Sausage and Egg Mc Muffin with hash browns. About two years ago I quit doing that. I stopped all fast food dieting. Since then I have been shopping at organic and natural foods stores. I am still over weight, but I can tell you for certain, I really do feel more healthy and a whole lot better everyday.

I can honestly say that without a doubt the food I'm buying there tastes a lot better too.

Lately, I've been thinking that our country had a great idea in the *"Victory Garden."* Maybe we should go back to growing our own. At least I know I can grow a tomato cheaper then $2.19. Not to mention I would know what I was eating.

GOD

CARE FOR THE SOUL

When you see the first flower of spring
Let your soul see it too
When you hear a symphony
The joy of jazz
The beat of rock and roll
Let your soul hear it too

When you smell the summer breeze
The mountain meadow
The seashore
Let your soul smell it too

When life brings sadness
Sorrow and pain
Share them with your soul
Let your soul be the light through the darkness
Let the wisdom flow
It will show the way

It's your soul that will remember
It's your soul that will stay
It's your soul that will show the way

What I am about to say may come as a great surprise to a lot of Christians and even to some of my family and friends: AMERICA IS NOT A CHRISTIAN COUNTRY. America is a secular democracy respecting the rights of its people to practice their religion without government interference. That's what our founding fathers meant for us and what hundreds of thousands of young men and women served their country for and a great many died for. That was the intention of the very First Amendment to the Constitution. There are those among us who would like to change this precedent and turn our country from a democracy into a theocracy. People like the Reverends Billy Graham and his son, Pat Robertson, Oral Roberts, John Hagee and many, many others. If any of them were selling anything other than religion, they would be either destitute or locked up in a mental hospital. Yet, they have access to our public airwaves, so thousands of Americans listen to their insane dogma and give them money every day. This is possible because the First Amendment gives them that right. It states, "Congress shall make no law respecting an establishment of religion or prohibiting the free exercise thereof: or abridging the freedom of speech." The far-right fundamentalists would very much like to establish a state religion, their own. They simply don't get it.

These so-called spiritual leaders have just two goals in life: make as much money as they can, mostly off of widows, orphans and tax relief; and turn America into a Christian state. They and their ministries are recipients of hundreds of millions of dollars in tax relief given to them on the condition that they do not participate in partisan political activities. Despite this fact, they engage daily in pursuit of their political goals. Republicans cater to and court the fundamentalist, right-wing Christian vote. When our nation's income tax laws were written, churches were exempt from income taxes on the condition that they refrain from participating in partisan political activities. It's perfectly okay for churches to encourage their flock to vote, which most mainline churches do, but it is not okay for churches to tell their flock who to vote for. If they want to do that, they have to give up their tax-exempt status and pay taxes like the rest of us. You can bet they are not going to do that.

With our current administration no federal agency like the IRS or Federal Communication Administration is going to enforce laws prohibiting tax-exempt churches from partisan political activities. In fact our government's "faith-based initiative" is giving our tax dollars to selected right-wing churches who in turn use that money to interfere with a woman's right to choose and to tell other Americans who they can and cannot marry. Any church or religion has a right to speak on issues important to them, but they do not have the right to enforce their will on the rest of us through taxpayer -funded programs. That's not why I and everyone I know put on the uniform to serve our country. We believed that if necessary we would give up our lives to protect our Constitution and the entire Bill of Rights, including the First Amendment and the rights of all religions. I have since learned that not everyone feels that way. While working at the Economic Development

Administration, I met an engineer who was a Fundamentalist Christian. Although he had never put on a uniform himself, he told me that he would never even consider giving up his life to protect my freedoms because I was going to hell anyway. I assured him that I was not going to hell; I knew that because there are four sins I have never committed. First, I have never murdered anyone; second, I have never committed a felony; third, I have never shopped at Wal-Mart; and fourth, not only have I not voted for a Republican, I have never even been tempted.

I hope that I am not leaving the impression that I am anti-religion because I am not. I hold in deepest respect all those religions that respect my right to believe whatever I choose to believe and otherwise leave me alone. That means, don't knock on my door, don't tell me who to vote for, don't tell my daughters they can't make their own decisions, and don't tell anyone who they can or cannot marry.

If the world's religious leaders insist on participating in world politics, then I have a suggestion. Since all wars have at last one religious component, (not counting Panama or Granada, which really were not wars per se), we should include them all, the pope, ministers, rabbis, ayatollahs, medicine men, monks, evangelical preachers, etc. We should invite the world's religious leaders to gather in an open-air stadium, lock them in, feed them nothing but bread and water, and don't let them out until they reach a peace agreement pledging to never go to war over religious ideology. Now there's an idea whose time has come.

In the beginning of this book I said that I didn't know where my soul came from or where it was going. I still don't. None of the world's religions, theologians or greatest thinkers can answer that question with absolute certainty; they can only point to "faith" as a possible answer. They may be right, I don't know. I certainly respect their right to their own understandings of faith.

For me faith is not fact, so I have been unable to find a plausible answer to the question of where I came from or where I am going. So I've concluded that what is really important is what we do in between, how we treat our families, our friends, other people, other nations, maybe someday other worlds and especially those who throw wakes across our bow. There was a popular Jackson Brown song in the early 70's, "Take It Easy," sung by the Eagles. One line in that song counsels, "Don't let the sound of your own wheels drive you crazy." I for one am trying hard to live by those words. I can think of no better way to honor my family and friends.

A GIFT FROM GARLIC GULCH

Many terrific people and things have come out of Garlic Gulch. Included among those terrific people and things would be Mike DeSantis and his Cucina DeSantis Restaurant located at First and Holgate in Seattle. Mike has asked me to share one of his favorite Italian recipes with everyone. His recipe makes for an ideal "romantic Italian dinner." Just add candlelight, fine Italian wine, romantic music from Italian singers like Enrico Caruso, Frank Sinatra, Dean Martin, Perry Como, Mario Lanza, Al Martino, Tony Bennett or Jerry Vale, some fresh roses, and the most terrific person in your life, and you will truly have a dinner to remember. Two other important reminders: first, you will get the very best results by shopping for ingredients at a store specializing in real Italian foods. Second, whenever possible choose organic and locally grown food products.

Here is the famous DeSantis family recipe for "DeSantis Italian Sausage Red Sauce":

¼ cup olive oil
2 cloves finely minced garlic
½ cup finely minced sweet onion
1 pound DeSantis Italian sausage (If you can't get Mike's sausage in particular, just make sure you get real Italian sausage.)

Cook above ingredients until halfway done.

2 28 oz cans imported San Marzano whole pear tomatoes in puree

Crush whole tomatoes in hand before placing into the pan with garlic, onion and sausage. Cook at medium-high heat for 20 minutes. In a separate pot, boil water to cook your favorite Italian spaghetti or other pasta according to directions. Once pasta is cooked, drain and add to the pan with sauce until pasta is well coated. Then add the following three ingredients on top:

5 fresh basil leaves cut into ribbons
½ cup grated romano
½ cup shredded mozzarella

Serve immediately with your favorite Italian wine, and you are transformed into a world famous chef! My favorite Italian wine is 2006 Centine Banfi from Toscana.

POSTSCRIPT

Earlier I asked "What do we have to be so smug about?" Well there are some people and things we have every right to be smug about. England has the English, Germany the Germans, Italy the Italians, China the Chinese, South America has Hispanics, but we have the *WORLD*. Among the soldiers in WWII who stormed the beaches at Anzio were Italian Americans. Among our soldiers who liberated Hitler's death camps were German Americans. America has more diversity than any other country in the world, and that is what has made us the greatest nation in the world.

Among Americans we have had George Washington, Thomas Jefferson, Lincoln, T. Roosevelt, F. Roosevelt, Harry Truman, D. Eisenhower, Lyndon Johnson, M.L. King and many, many others. We have led the world in science, industry, art, music, literature, etc. Most of all, our founding fathers gave us the two most valuable pieces of paper ever to come from the hand of man: the United States Constitution and Bill of Rights. Reagan and Bush Jr. have shredded these documents with deregulation, the Patriot Act and the Foreign Intelligence Surveillance Act. Our country's founding documents now require sewing back together, but we have hope. We have the opportunity to repair all the damage done to America and return to the status of a great nation. I am not sure another country in the world could do that. I'm looking forward to a time when I can travel the world and once again be proud to tell anyone, "I am an American, and I'm from Garlic Gulch."

Printed in the United States
207240BV00003B/1-105/P

9 781934 733226